Faithful, Focused, and Fearless is one of he time-liest labors of love you will read from now until you believe that you are just those things. Rev. Dr. Jo Ann Browning's encouraging words are divinely handcrafted to help you navigate these tough times and burst forth after the storms.

—YOLANDA ADAMS
DAUGHTER IN THE MINISTRY
GOSPEL ARTIST

Rev. Dr. Browning's newest book will inspire your spirit, calm your fears, and help you live a life that is empowered by faith. Her lessons provide the guidance you need to live your life to God's honor and glory, and to reap the benefits of His promises to you.

—DR. DOROTHY I. HEIGHT
CHAIR/PRESIDENT EMERITUS
NATIONAL COUNCIL OF NEGRO WOMEN
(BORN 3-24-1912 — DIED 4-20-2010)

In these days of chaos caused by the collapse of everything that is "important," we are desperately grateful for this instructional manual that teaches us lessons in future formation grounded in faith and lived without fear. I beg you—don't try to live life without it!

—DR. CAROLYN SHOWELL
BALTIMORE HEBREW UNIVERSITY

There comes a time when everyone must fight for their future. Dr. Jo Ann Browning presents a prolific power tool to help all of us fight the good fight of faith—and win! This is a must read.

—BISHOP VASHTI MURPHY MCKENZIE
AFRICAN METHODIST EPISCOPAL CHURCH

FAITHFUL, FOCUSED &

FEARLESS

JO ANN BROWNING, D.MIN.

CREATION
HOUSE

FAITHFUL, FOCUSED & FEARLESS *by* Rev. Dr. Jo Ann Browning
Published by Creation House Books
A Charisma Media Company
600 Rinehart Road
Lake Mary, Florida 32746
www.charismamedia.com

Unless otherwise marked, all Scripture quotations are from the Holy Bible, New International Version. Copyright © 1973, 1978, 1984, International Bible Society. Used by permission.

Scripture quotations marked KJV are from the King James Version of the Bible.

Design Director: Bill Johnson
Cover design by Nathan Morgan

Visit author's websites: www.ebenezerame.org, and www.drjabrowning.com

Library of Congress Control Number: 2010940919
International Standard Book Number: 978-1-61638-366-4
E-book ISBN: 978-1-61638-418-0

First Edition

11 12 13 14 15 — 9 8 7 6 5 4 3 2 1
Printed in Canada

TABLE OF CONTENTS

DEDICATION

*This book is dedicated to every faithful, focused, and
fearless woman (and woman-to-be), including:*

My grandmother, Mary Koontz
My mother, Ruth S. Leonard
My daughter, Candace Jo Ann Mary Browning
My mother-in-law, Esther A. Browning
My sisters-in-law, Cornelia Browning Moore and Carol Skaggs
My daughter-in-law, Courtney Riley Browning
My granddaughter, Kaylah Jo Ann Browning

ACKNOWLEDGMENTS

ONCE AGAIN, I want to thank God for the opportunity to teach and share with the women of Ebenezer A.M.E. Church and within the community of faith what the Lord has spoken to me on my journey, in my various roles as a wife, mother, grandmother, and serving in ministry with my husband, Rev. Dr. Grainger Browning, Jr., Senior Pastor for almost thirty years.

I want to thank my husband for his love, prayers, and support. I am eternally grateful for he has always encouraged me to be all that God wants me to be.

I also want to thank God for our son Grainger III, who continues to amaze us at how he faces challenges, fortified in the faith, and our daughter-in-law, Courtney and our beautiful and blessed grandchildren, Kaylah Jo Ann and Grainger IV. They have birthed something new and wonderful in our lives.

I want to thank God for our beautiful, brilliant, loving, creatively gifted, and discerning daughter, Candace, who continues to demonstrate wisdom beyond her years and has embraced her womanhood wisely. She has continued to teach me about life as I continue to teach her about how to sustain life as a woman.

I want to thank God for my beloved mother, Ruth Skaggs Leonard, who through her faith in God, has modeled for me how to pray without ceasing and to believe and trust God at all times.

I want to thank God for my deceased father, Henry Skaggs, who always made me think I was the best daughter in the world.

I want to thank God for my deceased stepfather, James Leonard, who was loving and supportive.

I want to thank God for my only brother, Timothy S. Skaggs, his wife, Carol and my nephews Tim and Adam, who have now stepped into young-adult manhood with ease and integrity.

I want to thank my in-laws Dr. Grainger Browning, Sr., Mrs. Esther Browning, and Elder Cornelia Browning Moore.

I want to thank Dr. Irene Owens, Dean of Library and Information Science at North Carolina Central University in Durham, North Carolina.

I want to thank our Executive Assistant, Sis. Katie Bostic and the Assistant Executive Assistant, Sis. Lee Epps.

I want to thank my circle of beloved sister-friends for your love and prayers.

I want to thank Courtney Smith Brown, my editor and publishing agent, who is used by God to not only edit, but to encourage me to continue the journey to provide written help for women.

I want to thank Charisma Media and Creation House, and Robert Caggiano and particularly the professional assistance of Brenda Davis.

I also want to thank Kim Cassell for her prayers and teaching me how to use the computer to get this book written.

I also want to thank Trish Smith and Rev. Chandra Marriott for reviewing the manuscript.

I want to thank Sis. Patty Haynes Lee for her constant help and encouragement, and the Ministry of Helps of Ebenezer AME Church.

I want to thank the historical women I have read about and have admired over the years: Harriet Tubman, Sojourner Truth, Mary McCloud Bethune, Ida B. Wells, Barbara Jordan, Coretta Scott King, Shirley Chisholm, Dr. Dorothy Height, and all of the women in the belly of the slave ships who held on and did not give up and still encourage me.

Finally, I sincerely thank God for all of those who have called out my name in prayer as I have tried to do my best on this journey of faith. If I have missed saying thank you to anyone who has helped me on this journey of birthing this book, please charge it to my head and not my heart.

FOREWORD

ERHAPS IN ALL fairness, this most recent publication of Dr. JoAnn Browning should be packaged in bright yellow C.S.I. "caution" tape. Every fear, false impression, self-righteous, self-imposed delusion or distraction falls victim to her "sword of the spirit." Anyone embracing the title becomes a prophetic "suspect." *Faithful, Focused, and Fearless* is a Christian labyrinth that leads the pilgrim on an interior circuitous path to soul healing, discovery, and liberation. The author is a trustworthy guide.

In placing her own life and story under the scrutiny of the scriptures, she compels the reader to do the same. Transparency, candor, and openness are not easy to come by. With each step (chapter) we gain a profound sense of our nearness to or distance from kingdom authenticity. This is the treasure, the "pearl of great price." Those given to procrastination, distraction, denial, or codependent religion will experience the fresh wind of amazement. If you have been purpose aware in your journey, your wings will be enlarged. Your heart renewed.

Dr. Browning's "Spiritual Solutions" engage the "depths of the revelation knowledge of God." Radical life principles hosting one's past, present, and future emerge with unbridled courage. And the residue of girl-child hopes and deferred dreams are ignited with creative fire. It comes to you that you still have the power! The power of choice. You are not "stuck," "finished," or "over!" You still have the power to shape your future. "Wow!" You are positioned for prophetic realization. And Dr. JoAnn Browning is the kingdom agency of your royal induction. Welcome to your destiny! Welcome to your self. Welcome home.

—REV. DR. CECELIA WILLIAMS BRYANT
SENIOR EPISCOPAL SUPERVISOR
AFRICAN METHODIST EPSICOPAL CHURCH

PROLOGUE

BEING FAITHFUL MEANS to be consistently trustworthy and loyal, especially to a person, promise, or duty; being focused means to concentrate effort or attention on a particular thing; and, being fearless means to be resolute in the face of dangers or challenges. My mom is the epitome of all these characteristics.

As a young adult, my mom was accepted into Boston University (BU). Even though she didn't have the money to attend BU, she had to be faithful to God that He would make a way. As a result of faithfulness, her tuition was paid every year for the four years she attended BU. Even though there were not many African-American female students at BU, my mom stayed focused. To attend a university such as BU, you have to be fearless. Every day my mom had to overcome racism from teachers who were expecting her to fail.

At the age of thirty-five, my mom accepted the call into ministry and attended Howard University Divinity School. Even though she did not fully understand what God had in store for her she was faithful to God's plan for her life. She was focused while she attended divinity school. Not only was she in a demanding program, she was also married with one child, pregnant with me, and working a full-time job. My mom was fearless when accepting the call into ministry because during that time women preachers were not acknowledged as "real" preachers; but, my mom was fearless to the world and did what God told her to do.

This book, *Faithful, Focused, and Fearless: Lessons to Fortify Your Future*, is a collection of tried-and-true lessons that my mom learned and applied in her life. When I was a child, I overlooked the advantage of applying my mom's life lessons and brushed them off because she was my mother. Now that I am older, I can't get enough of the learning opportunities from our mother-daughter talks. Do not make the same mistake and brush these lessons off like I did when I was younger. Please do not pass up reading this book, and please do not miss your opportunity to take advantage of these lessons.

—CANDACE JO ANN MARY BROWNING
(DAUGHTER OF AUTHOR)

PREFACE

IN MY WIFE's first book, *Our Savior, Our Sisters, Ourselves,* she focused on the spiritual and historical importance of women in the Bible and in society. Even though the focus of the book was women, it captured a universal truth of how faith in God allows us all to achieve far beyond what we could have ever hoped or imagined. In this second book, my wife takes that premise to the next level by allowing you, the reader, to discover the qualities and traits that are required to be all that God is calling you to be.

The following lessons allow you to see the deeper meaning of God's Word and its practical applications for your own life. In many ways, my wife is sharing her own journey as one of the pioneers of female co-pastors. She has been *faithful, focused, and fearless* and has stood strong against all odds to come out victorious on the other side as a wife, mother, grandmother, daughter, sister, aunt, friend, and a woman of God. She keeps all of these responsibilities in perfect balance.

I pray that as you read these inspiring, profound lessons you will discover to a greater extent the Christ who resides in you, and in doing so, you will embrace what I love about my wife of more than thirty-one years, that if you are faithful, focused, and fearless God will not only bless you, but He will also bless those closest to you.

I never could have become all that God has blessed me to be without a faithful, focused, and fearless woman of God by my side. To God be the glory for the great things He has done, is doing, but most of all for the things He is yet to do, for the best is yet to come!

—REV. DR. GRAINGER BROWNING, JR.
SENIOR PASTOR, EBENEZER A.M.E. CHURCH
(HUSBAND OF AUTHOR)

INTRODUCTION

D o you trust God? If your answer is "yes," then what
are you afraid of? What is keeping you from living a life
that is fortified and blessed?

Trust and fear cannot coexist. The choice is yours. You can
make a conscious decision to trust God and live free and on purpose, or you can choose to live a limited life in which you are
controlled by fear. My purpose in writing this book was to com-
pel you to choose to trust God and live the boundless life that He
created you to live.

To be faithful, you must be focused. If you're not focused on
God, any little issue that rears its head in your life will cause your
spiritual knees to buckle and your faith to waver. Once you're
focused, once you're mind is attuned to the voice of God, there
will be nothing that can make you doubt Him. You'll be focused
and faithful. Then, whatever limits you have placed upon yourself will be eliminated, and the enemy will never be able to stop
you in your tracks again.

Once you realize just how powerful God is, and that His
power is greater than any force on this earth, you will come full
circle, and you will no longer be afraid. God desires us to be *faithful, focused, and fearless.* Therefore, He has given me eleven lessons
to give to you, to help you learn to live a life without limits:

- Lesson 1: Embrace Your God-Given Opportunities
- Lesson 2: Get into God's Presence
- Lesson 3: Believe God Will Turn It Around For Your Good
- Lesson 4: Submit to God's Will for Your Life
- Lesson 5: Remember God's Promises
- Lesson 6: Refuse to Give up
- Lesson 7: Trust God to Take Care of You
- Lesson 8: Stand Still and See the Victory

- Lesson 9: Be Willing to Change
- Lesson 10: Wait With an Expectant Spirit
- Lesson 11: Reclaim Your Joy

I believe God gave me these lessons to give to you based on the spiritual gifts in 1 Corinthians 12:8–10, including: "To one there is given through the Spirit the message of wisdom, to another the message of knowledge by means of the same Spirit, to another faith by the same Spirit, to another gifts of healing by that one Spirit, to another miraculous powers, to another prophecy, to another distinguishing between spirits, to another speaking in different kinds of tongues, and to still another the interpretation of tongues."

I wrote this book as a tool for you to use to literally change your life and unlock your spiritual gifts. This book is much more than a good read. After each lesson, you will find five exercises that will help you develop spiritual solutions to complement the lesson you just learned. The key word in that sentence is *learned*. If you are not able to honestly answer each of the Spiritual Solutions, you need to re-read the lesson and contemplate it again. The Spiritual Solutions are designed to help you open up, examine yourself, and develop an action plan for your life.

Keep your Bible handy, as I refer to Scripture throughout this text. I encourage you to read your Word, along with this book, to truly unleash the power of God in your life.

This is no time to fear. Are you ready? Get your Bible, get a pen, and get away to a quiet place. We've got work to do.

Lesson 1

EMBRACE YOUR
GOD-GIVEN OPPORTUNITIES

TRUST ME, YOU are not the only one who is afraid. Things are tough right now, and we have all, in one way or another, wondered if we will make it through. The country is in a recession, unemployment is at a record high, foreclosures are on the rise, there are wars and rumors of war, natural disasters are becoming more commonplace, and new diseases threaten us on a regular basis—it's easy to feel afraid during these times. It's a fact of life—you will endure trials and tribulations; but, if you are willing to trust God, He will show you the purpose of the process.

I have journeyed with God long enough to realize that times like these are really blessed opportunities for God's people to grow in faith. This is no time to give in to fear—now is the time for you to take your faith and your confidence in God to the next level.

It's time for you to embrace who you are in Christ Jesus and whose you are in the Lord. When you are unclear about where your strength comes from, you begin to compromise and reach out for worldly solutions. When you're not sure that you can make it, you tend to turn away from God and you start to seek guidance from friends, co-workers, family members, even strangers. It is critical that you stay in touch with God in times of trouble.

When you find yourself in the midst of a crisis, it is imperative that you take a moment to get honest with yourself and seek Christ. When you know how to tap into the power of Christ that lives on the inside of you, you will know in your spirit, on the inside, that everything is going to be all right. You will land on your feet. God will enable you to go through and get over your problems.

I wrote this chapter specifically to encourage your troubled soul. The Lord wants you to face your problems from a perspective of empowerment. You might feel beat down because of what you've been going through. But God wants you to realize that you are a conqueror in Christ. Right now, you may feel so discouraged that all you want to do is give up. My prayer is that this chapter will encourage you. Don't give up; don't get weak. Refuse to compromise—this is your blessed opportunity to believe and trust that God will turn your situation around.

> **Keep telling yourself: "I am a
> conqueror, and I shall triumph over
> this thing and have the victory."
> Before long, you'll believe it.**

God knows that the enemy is trying to destroy you. You need to know that because of who you are in the Lord Jesus Christ, you shall conquer the enemy. This time you will not shrink. This time you will not be defeated. You will not fear. You will not compromise. This time you shall conquer the thing that has been threatening to destroy you.

Consider Romans 8, Paul had never been to Rome when he wrote this letter around A.D. 58. Rome was one of the most powerful cities in the world. Paul pours out his spirit because he wanted to convey the very essence of his faith and belief, even though his opponents were busy spreading lies against him. Paul's epistle to the Christian church in Rome was powerful, profound, and prophetic. Clearly, even though he was in the midst of a personal crisis, Paul was clear about who he was and whose he was.

God wants to develop a *Paul-esque* strength in you. He wants to see you become so strong in your faith, that no matter what personal trials you may encounter, you will have a steadfast assurance that the Lord will come through for you. He wants you to realize that you can still experience His grace and mercy, even though you feel as though you are sitting in a hellhole.

The Lord will be with you through the midst of it all. This is no time for fear.

No matter what you're facing, this is your blessed opportunity to be victorious. The enemy might be messing with you on one level, or you might be facing a multifaceted attack. He could be messing with:

- your family
- your marriage
- your children
- your finances
- your employment
- your home
- your health
- your hope and joy
- your purpose
- your peace of mind

When you are on task and working toward your purpose, you can expect that the enemy will turn up the heat and intensify his attack on you. When the enemy is messing with your faith, you feel discouraged and disappointed, defeated and overwhelmed, stressed and confused, discombobulated and fearful. You begin to feel lost. When the enemy really intensifies his attack against you, you may even begin to wonder, "Is Jesus real in my soul? Will He really make a difference in my life?"

If you've been contemplating those questions, it is time for you to declare and decree, in the midst of the mess, in the midst of the battles and problems in your life: "I shall conquer this thing and I shall have the victory." You truly are more than a conqueror, and this time the enemy will not have his way with you. This time you will exercise the authority of the Holy Spirit. This time you will speak to the problem and the battle in faith and believe and trust God. This time, you will stop the enemy dead in his tracks.

Paul was trying to encourage the church in Rome to embrace who they were in the Lord Jesus Christ. There were Jews who rejected Jesus and did not believe that He was the Messiah, the Son of the most high God. So in the beginning of chapter 8, Paul was emphasizing the importance of living our lives in the Spirit of Christ Jesus. The Holy Spirit, the Spirit of Christ in you, will sanctify you and restore you when you fall.

In this life, you will struggle with sin, but you can have victory over sin and death in Jesus Christ. The Holy Spirit gives you what you need to triumph over your flesh. In other words, the Holy Spirit will quicken your mortal body. *Quicken* in Greek means to "make alive." When the Holy Spirit comes, it quickens you. It makes you feel alive. It gives you the sense that you can endure. Christ in you gives you life within, even though the situation you may be in looks dead.

In Romans 8:18, Paul informs the reader of the reality of suffering. You are not exempt from suffering because you're saved. Paul writes, "Our present sufferings are not worth comparing with the glory that will be revealed in us." That ought to encourage you—it means that the glory to come will far exceed the sufferings of the present. Then Paul writes in verse 28, "In all things, God works for the good of those who love him, who have been called according to his purpose." There should be no questioning that God will intervene to help sustain you.

Paul then starts a crescendo of rhetorical questions. In verse 31, he writes, "What, then, shall we say in response to this?" He answers himself with a rhetorical question, "If God is for us, who can be against us?" As a Christian, the reality is, the enemy will come against you with all of his force, his malice, his imps, and his skills. He wants to keep you from reaching your full potential. However, whatever God wants for you, whatever God plans for you, whatever God's purpose is for you—God is for you!

So, if God is for you, and you truly believe that, then who can possibly be against you? You shall conquer this thing and have victory. You serve a God who is on the side of His people. Be assured in the Lord. Be encouraged in the Lord. Rest in the knowledge that no weapon formed against you shall prosper. God is for you. God has called you for a specific purpose within His kingdom. God loved you so much that He gave His only begotten Son. God has redeemed you through Jesus Christ. God has justified you.

In verse 35, Paul asks, "Who shall separate us from the love of Christ? Shall trouble or hardship or persecution or famine or nakedness or danger or sword? Who shall separate us from the love of Christ?" If you believe, you will not face any danger that can separate us from Jesus. As a child of God, there is no concern that can distance you from Jesus. When you have a steadfast trust and belief in God, there is not a person or a circumstance that has the power to separate you from God. So even if you lose your job, your home, or even your marriage, you will not be separated from the God who works all things together for your good.

I know you don't want to go through it, but take comfort in the fact that whatever you go through, you shall overcome. You are a conqueror in Jesus Christ through the power of the Holy Spirit. No matter what the enemy tries to do to you, the Holy Spirit will provide power to sustain you, keep you, and protect you until your victory comes.

When you feel your faith weakening, be like Paul and declare as he did in verses 38–39, "For I am convinced that neither death nor life, neither angels nor demons, neither the present nor the future, nor any powers, neither height nor depth, nor anything else in all creation, will be able to separate us from the love of God that is in Christ Jesus our Lord." You can't be scared and convinced. When you are convinced of something, you are certain. When you are certain of the outcome, there is no need for you to be afraid.

In Christ, you are more than a conqueror because you have the power of the Holy Spirit to resist the devil. You will prevail over your problem. You'll go through the fire, but you won't get burned. You'll be in the floods, but you won't drown. You'll face some giants, but you will not be afraid. God will take care of you. When you overcome your problems, you'll be able to testify:

- God healed my body.
- God restored my finances.
- God made my business prosper.
- God reunited my marriage.
- God saved my children.
- God gave me a better home than the one I lost in foreclosure.

Do you see where I'm going? You and I serve a God that can do anything but fail. All you have to do to activate God's power in your life is to walk in the power of the Holy Spirit of the most high God. What God has for you is for you. Take authority over your fear. Look the enemy in the eye and declare your victory in advance, "I am a conqueror, and I already have the victory."

I cannot reiterate this point enough: this is your blessed opportunity to tap into the Christ in you and rise above your fear. If you do, I guarantee you, your response to trials and tribulations will be different. The next time you face trouble, and trust me, there will be a next time, you will not run from it. You will not give in to fear. You will not crumble. Why? Because you know that if God brought you through before, He can do it again. You were happy before; you'll be happy again. You had peace of mind before; you'll have peace of mind again.

You can't conquer anything without God's power working within you.

The truly amazing thing is that with God, you are *more* than a conqueror. That means when you get to the other side of the problem, God has additional blessings, over and beyond what you've conquered. So if you've lost your job, your home, or your finances during these times, you ought to believe that an even better job, home, and greater prosperity are just on the other side, because you are more than a conqueror.

SPIRITUAL SOLUTIONS

1. Tap into the Spirit power within yourself. Tell the enemy, "I'm more than a conqueror." Write down five areas within your life in which you are taking control back from the devil.

_____

_____

_____

_____

_____

2. Dispel the lies the enemy has whispered in your spiritual ear. Tell yourself about those things, "I have victory in Christ Jesus. I shall conquer because of the Holy Spirit." Write down some of the lies that the enemy has whispered in your ear, and declare what you know to be true about yourself.

_____

_____

_____

_____

_____

3. Thank God for being there. God has always been with you in all of your struggles, all of your problems, and all of your concerns. Write down some of your most challenging problems and how God brought you through each one of them.

_____

_____

_____

_____

_____

4. Find a faith connection with someone you trust. Write the names, numbers, and e-mail addresses of a few people who will pray for you, without judgment, in the midst of your concerns.

_____

_____

_____

_____

_____

5. Do a self-check. Write down how you feel about Jesus while you are in the midst of crisis. Do you feel like He is close, or do you feel far away from Him? Why?

_____

_____

_____

_____

_____

Lesson 2

GET INTO GOD'S PRESENCE

WHEN I FIND myself questioning God, I grab my Bible and do some "shero" research. I look for lessons from the biblical female heroes of the day. There are certain women in the Word of God, whose stories serve to empower women today. The Shunammite woman is one of those women. She is one of my favorite women because she dealt with her realities without hesitation and without reservation. In other words, she did what she had to do. I want you to focus on her character as a woman, and try to identify places within yourself that might need to be strengthened.

Her story begins with a visit from the prophet Elisha, who has traveled to Shunem. The Bible does not give her name. She is only referred to by the fact that she is an inhabitant of Shunem. But she's not just an ordinary Shunammite woman; the Bible defines her as a "well-to-do woman."

The first characteristic that the Bible ascribes to her is that she was financially comfortable. The Bible does not identify her wealth with her husband. She was independently wealthy. She was married, but she was independently wealthy. The Word mentions her wealth before mentioning that she's married. She had her own resources. As a woman, it is OK for you to obtain, develop, and create your own resources. If you and your spouse have decided to combine your resources, that's wonderful if that is the agreement. However, it is imperative that you have the ability to create your own options.

The Bible also tells us that she was kind, gracious, and hospitable. The prophet Elisha would stop, eat, and rest at her house whenever he visited Shunem. She was also wise and spiritually intuitive. She recognized that Elisha was "a holy man of God," and she encouraged her husband to make a room for the prophet so that he could have a comfortable stay whenever he came to visit (2 Kings 4:9–10).

Her husband honored, respected, and supported her decision. There was no indication of any discussion, no tension; there was not one question from her husband regarding her plan. She used her godly influence to do what she needed to do and what she heard God say to her in her spirit. Her husband trusted her decision.

Second Kings 4:11–13 reads as follows: "One day when Elisha came, he went up to his room and lay down there. He said to his servant Gehazi, 'Call the Shunammite.' So he called her, and she stood before him. Elisha said to him, 'Tell her, "You have gone to all this trouble for us. Now what can be done for you?"'"

She was obedient. When the prophet called her, she came. She stood before him, which is a sign of reverence. She recognized that he was a man of God. Elisha wanted to bless her because she had been so gracious to him.

It is time to start doing things from your heart. If you are looking for something in return, you have got the wrong motive.

She was content. Initially, she refuses Elisha's offer. She remarks that she has a home, and she is surrounded by her people. She didn't want anything. Remember, she was financially stable. She did not have a hidden agenda. Elisha wanted to do something for her because she was kind, sensitive, and willing to share her resources.

Have you ever revealed your compassionate, sensitive, kindhearted side to someone who did not appreciate it? Have you ever given the very best of yourself to someone else and they never even said "thank you?" God wants to heal that hurt so that you don't become insensitive and cold. God wants you to reclaim the sensitivity of your womanhood and reclaim that part of you that you may have shut down because it was not appreciated. God wants to bless you with unexpected blessings, but He can't do it if you are shut down because somebody was insensitive to you.

Even though the Shunammite woman politely declined, Elisha still wanted to bless her. So he asked his servant to find out the true desires of her heart. For a Jewish woman to not have a child was viewed negatively. It was particularly shameful not to have a son. It turns out by her second response, that she really wanted a son. But the reality was that her husband was too old to impregnate her.

I want you to know this my sister, God knows what we desire in our hearts, and He has the power and the resources to give it to us. Don't ever forget that fact. You don't have to speak it to anybody. God knows what you desire, even if you have not spoken a word about it to anyone.

So, Elisha calls her again and speaks prophetically, telling her that this time next year, she would have a son in her arms. She objected, thinking the prophet was misleading her. It wasn't her lack of faith that made her object; I think she was initially surprised that Elisha knew her private prayers. For that prayer to be answered was almost unbelievable for her. But she did become pregnant the next year and gave birth to a son, just as Elisha said she would.

> *Some things are between you and God only. God is ready and is capable to give you the desires of your heart if you are willing to trust and believe.*

That's just how God works. As you read this book, you ought to believe that God wants to give you the desires of your heart.

If it's a child, it's yours. If it's a home, it's yours. If it's a husband, it's yours. If it's a business, it's yours. If it's a promotion, it's yours.

In verses 18–20, the Bible declares the child grew. One day he was out in the field reaping the harvest with his father, and he suffered a sunstroke. His father told his servant to carry the boy to his mother. He didn't know what to do, how to deal with it, or how to handle it. He must have known his wife could handle it, because she was a strong, confident, competent woman.

The boy sat on his mother's lap until noon, and then he died. Her only child, the child she desired died in her arms. All was going well. Life was wonderful, and then her worst nightmare happens. My sister, no matter how wonderful and kind and loving you may be, you are not exempt from a nightmare experience. The question is, how do you deal with it?

She was wise; she knew where her help came from. She didn't weep and wail; she didn't scream and holler. In verse 21, the Bible says, she calmly went up and laid her son on the bed of the man of God and shut the door. Then she calls her husband, and she tells him what she needs. She didn't ask him—she just tells him. "Please send me one of the servants and a donkey so I can go to the man of God quickly and return" (2 Kings 4:22).

She was certain. Her husband initially questions her because there are only certain times you're supposed to go see the prophet, and the time was not right. I can imagine him saying to her, "I'm bringing the donkey and the servant, but honey, you aren't supposed to be doing this." But the Shunammite woman knew what she had to do and when she had to do it. She tells her husband, "It shall be well."

> ### In the midst of her worst nightmare, she knew all she had to do was get to the man of God.

When you find yourself in the midst of the storm, get to God. Reach for God—even if your friends or family don't understand or don't agree with your decision. Get yourself in the face of God. Do not reach out or turn to the ungodly when your problem needs the strength of God. Get to God with a steadfast faith that God has the power to restore, revive, renew, return, and release your blessing back unto you.

She was determined. In verses 24–25, the Bible declares that she saddled the donkey and told the servant to lead the way to Mount Carmel. She instructed him not to slow down, unless she told him to. My sister, when you find yourself in the midst of a nightmare, you have to be faithful and steadfast. Be assertive and aggressive in the faith. God will give you the strength to overcome.

When you need a breakthrough, you've got to be prepared to go fast and go hard for the things of God. When you are pursuing a breakthrough, wavering is not an option. Getting to the other side of your nightmare requires you to be focused. It's as simple as this: stay focused on God and He will bless you.

In verse 26, Elisha sees her approaching from afar. He told his servant to go out and meet her and ask her three specific questions:

1. Are you all right?
2. Is your husband all right?
3. Is your child all right?

You can see she was faithful simply by how she responds to: "Everything is all right." The King James Version says, "It is well." She speaks faith even though all hell is breaking loose in her life. But there's something else, she was wise. She knew that Elisha's servant, Gehazi could not help her. She had come to see the man of God. There was no need for her to waste her time talking to Gehazi about her problem.

> *Don't waste your time talking to the wrong people. Your girlfriend can't help you when all hell breaks loose in your life. Get to Jesus.*

God wants to work something out in your life, but you

keep going to the wrong resources and seeking what you need in the wrong direction. Stop wasting your energy, your time, and your breath on useless, unproductive resources. Seek God's face while He might be found. Seek first His kingdom and His righteousness, and all these things will be given to you as well. (See Matthew 6:33.)

The Shunammite woman was forthright. When she got to the man of God, the one who could help her, Gehazi tries to push her away; but Elisha tells him to leave her alone. Elisha, the man of God, recognizes her distress. Don't you know that God sees you in distress? God recognizes when you're going through something. In verse 28, she tells Elisha what has happened plainly and confidently, "Did I ask you for a son, my lord?" she said. "Didn't I tell you, 'Don't raise my hopes'?"

Like the Shunammite woman, you have to speak to God honestly. Think about it, if He knows every strand of hair on your head, don't you think He knows how you really feel? He is just waiting for you to be honest with Him. If you are not honest with God about where you are, how you feel, and what you're going through, He may not be able to entrust you with what He has for you. He is looking for you to be open and honest.

She was tenacious. She knows that she came too far to give up now. She realizes that she is on the cusp of her breakthrough. In verses 30–31, the Shunammite woman reaches the ultimate place of faith. When Elisha sends Gehazi to lay his staff on her son, I can imagine her saying to Elisha, "I'm not going anywhere until you leave with me. Did you hear what I said?" She refuses to give up.

My sister, don't give up on the cusp of the breakthrough. The cusp is the very place before the breakthrough and the turn-around. It is the very place that you have to press harder. Don't give in to the devastation of the nightmare you might be facing. Don't give up hope; don't lose faith. You've come too far to turn back now.

She was relentless. Gehazi returns to tell them that the boy has not awakened. The staff didn't make a difference. The

Shunammite woman knew that the staff would not work. She knew that her son needed the power of the man of God, and she wasn't moving until the man of God went with her. So Elisha got up and followed her.

> *You must have persistent faith and believe*
> *God for supernatural, life-changing*
> *power to overcome a dead situation.*

When Elisha arrived, he went up to his room. The dead boy was on the bed. Elisha shut the door. He lay on top of the body, mouth-to-mouth, eye-to-eye, hand-to-hand. The body grew warm and life began to return. Elisha got up and he walked back and forth for a while. Then he stretched out on the body a second time. The boy sneezed seven times and opened his eyes. God is on top of your situation, and he is breathing new life into your dead places. God has the power. God is a restorer. God can do it for you.

The Shunammite woman appears again in 2 Kings 8:1–6. Elisha advised her and her family to leave Shunem because a seven-year famine was imminent. God is calling you to be obedient to His voice.

She was obedient. For seven years, she did what the man of God said and lived in the land of the Philistines. After seven years, she returned to her homeland. In the meantime, Gehazi (I love how God works!) was telling the king in Shunem about all the great things the prophet Elisha had done. As Gehazi was telling him about the Shunamite woman's son, in walks the Shunammite woman and her son at just the right time.

She had come to beg the king to restore her resources (her house and her land). Her husband had died; she was a single mother. She verified the story about her son, and the king restored everything to her, plus interest! "Give back everything that belonged to her, including all the income from her land from the day she left the country until now" (2 Kings 8:1–6). My sister, God wants to restore everything that the enemy has taken from you and more. God wants to restore your confidence, your joy, your sensitivity, your strength, and your wisdom. Whatever you lost, due to one of life's midnights and nightmares, God will restore it unto you.

God said He will restore. He said He will restore, and He will give you the desires of your heart. He's done it before, and he'll do it again. He's faithful. He's true. He cannot lie. You're in a win-win situation with God.

Spiritual Solutions

1. Look in the mirror. What characteristics do your share with the Shunammite woman? Are you steadfast and consistent? Sensitive and sincere? Why or why not? Write down the steps you will take to become a strong and steady woman.

_____

_____

_____

_____

_____

2. Leave it alone. Be honest with yourself, should the dead things in your life stay dead? Are you in a dead-end job? Is your relationship ever going to go to the next level? Are you harboring hurt from the past? What dead things are still living with you and keeping you from experiencing the deeper things of God?

_____

_____

_____

_____

_____

3. Examine your options. Are you living your life to please others because they are providing things for you? Wouldn't you like to at least have some say in your destiny? If you could create your own options, write down the things you would do differently?

_____

_____

_____

_____

_____

FAITHFUL, FOCUSED & FEARLESS

4. Get honest with yourself. Do you believe God is pleased with how you are living your life? In what areas do you need God to increase your faith? What things are you willing to do differently to get to God?

_____

_____

_____

_____

_____

5. Ask God to restore it. What have you lost that you need God to restore? Your finances? Your home? Your self-esteem? Your mind? Write down the things that you believe God can restore in your life. (Check your list; don't ask God to restore what you know should stay dead.)

_____

_____

_____

_____

_____

Lesson 3

BELIEVE GOD WILL TURN IT AROUND FOR YOUR GOOD

ARE YOU FACING a lingering problem that is creating havoc in your life? Some problems in life can nag at your spirit and invade your thoughts at the most unexpected times. Not only can problems be irritating, they can also be debilitating. A serious, unresolved problem can roadblock your purpose in life, because it interferes with your desires. It ambushes your abilities and destroys your passion.

God is able to remove that problem from your life. It doesn't matter what your problem is—sickness, financial uncertainty, relationship troubles, problem children—no matter what you are facing, God will turn it around for your good.

God has the power to get you over and through the worst of times. So before you throw in the towel and decide to walk away, give God a chance to work a miracle in the midst of your difficulty and devastation. Now is not the time to give up on God. You may be wondering, "Will God ever come through for me?" You need to know that this phase in your life represents a transition. God is moving you to a place where you will know and embrace the deeper things of God. In this period of transition, you must take control of your thoughts; banish all fear, doubt, and reservation, and begin to trust and believe that God will turn your situation around for your good.

We serve a God who specializes in turnaround power. In order for you to tap into that power, you must be willing to trust God in this season of your life. Joseph's story is a clear example of God's turnaround power. The story of Joseph reminds us that regardless of how life may unfold, we serve a sovereign God whose providence always prevails. It illustrates how God really is in control even in the worst of times. I love this story because in the end, we learn some things about God's ways. His ways are always:

- purposeful
- reliable
- dependable
- certain and secure

That should be comforting to you, because it means that no matter what someone else's actions or opinions are toward you are, they cannot interfere with what God intends for your life. It is all irrelevant. God is in control, and He has the power to turn anything around.

Joseph was Jacob's baby. He was his father's favorite child, and his coat of many colors was tangible evidence of that fact. As a result, his brothers hated him. They hated him so much, they could not even speak peaceably to him or say a kind word. Joseph was also a dreamer and he could interpret dreams. God showed him how he would someday be in power over his family. When Joseph shared the dream with his father and his brothers, they rebuked him (Genesis 37:5–10). Although his brothers were jealous of what he'd told them, Jacob observed what his son said and kept it in his mind.

God may speak to you through your dreams. What are you dreaming of?

One day, Jacob sent Joseph out to check on his brothers who were feeding the flocks. Joseph, in his coat of many colors, the favorite son, the dreamer, the interpreter, pressed his way out to find his brothers. The Bible states that when they saw him far off, they began to collaborate and conspire against him. They wanted to kill him, but one of his brothers, Reuben, convinced them against killing Joseph. (He had planned to rescue Joseph later.) So they decided to cast him into a pit. When Joseph arrived, that's just what they did. While his brothers sat around eating, a group of Midianites came along and saw Joseph in the pit. Joseph's brothers sold him to the Ishmaelites for twenty pieces of silver. When Reuben returned to the pit, Joseph was gone. The Bible states that the brothers dipped Joseph's coat of many colors in goat's blood. They took the coat to Jacob and told him that Joseph had been devoured by a beast.

Many years pass in Egypt. Joseph, the dreamer, was wrongly imprisoned, but his gift made a way for him and he found favor with the warden. In Genesis 39:23, the Bible says, "The warden paid no attention to anything under Joseph's care, because the Lord was with Joseph and gave him success in whatever he did." Know that God can grant you favor in any and every situation. The amazing thing about God's favor is that it is compounded, meaning there are times when God's favor multiplies. Joseph's relationship with the warden, through God's favor, ultimately led him to receiving favor with Pharaoh. The key point I need you to understand is that God's favor, not man's, has power. Don't waste your time living to please man—live your life to please God, and watch His favor be manifested in your life. Years passed before Joseph received Pharaoh's (favor), but he did not falter in the midst of his wait. After all that he had been through, Joseph still put his trust and faith, not in Pharaoh, but in God.

A severe famine had seized Egypt and the surrounding areas. Joseph's brothers journeyed to Egypt in search of food. Although they came face-to-face with Joseph, they did not recognize him. But Joseph recognized them. Joseph's brothers came and bowed down before him, with their faces to the earth, just like the dream had shown Joseph in the beginning. The dream that Joseph had in chapter 37 now begins to unfold.

Joseph, who they thought was dead, discloses his identity to his brothers with tears streaming down his face. In Genesis 45:4–5, Joseph says, "Come close to me.... I am your brother Joseph, the one you sold into Egypt! And now, do not be distressed and do not be angry with yourselves for selling me here, because it was to save lives that God sent me ahead of you." God had made Joseph lord over Pharaoh's house and ruler throughout all the land of Egypt. God superseded Joseph's brothers' guilt and fear and resolved his father's years of grief. Joseph sought no revenge. He realized his purpose.

Joseph's story is a shining example of God's miraculous, wonder-working power. You should know beyond a shadow of a doubt that God is at work in your life. God is always working it out for His purpose and for His good.

In his book *Church Dogmatics*, Karl Barth writes that there is a "dialectical reality" in God. That means God does His own work at the same time; He honors the work of His creation. The sovereignty of God created a newness for Joseph and his family. The mood of God and the unfolding of Joseph's story negates and cancels the past, redefines the present, and opens up the future. It is evidence that God can and will turn things around for your good.

In chapter 50, Joseph's father is dead, and even though Joseph had already assured his brothers that he had forgiven them, they needed to hear it one more time. In verses 19–21, Joseph says to them, "Don't be afraid. Am I in the place of God? You intended to harm me, but God intended it for good to accomplish what is now being done, the saving of many lives. So then, don't be afraid. I will provide for you and your children."

Clearly, God had turned Joseph's brothers' potential tragedy into triumph. His brothers had planned for evil by selling Joseph into slavery, but God planned it for good. In other words, in the midst of their plans, God's plan was hidden but working for good all along. The Bible is replete with examples of how God turned what was meant for evil, into good:

- Shadrach, Meshach, and Abednego were cast into a fiery furnace, but they were not burned.
- Daniel was thrown into the lion's den, but God locked the lion's jaws.
- Little David killed the massive Goliath with stone and a slingshot.

The ultimate turnaround occurred when Jesus came on the scene. They thought they had Him; the enemy was on His trail. But He had a divine assignment from God. They hung Him high and stretched Him wide. He hung His head and then He died. The enemy thought he had Him. But on the third day, He got up with all power.

My sisters, be assured that God will turn it around for you, too. Be determined to live your life faithful, focused, and fearless. Don't worry about what your enemies are planning behind your back. You must walk in faith. Don't walk around afraid that you might get laid off; don't walk around afraid that he might leave you; don't walk around afraid that you'll lose your home. Walk confidently, fully assured by God, that if any one of these things do happen, God will work it out for your good. You must live a life that is connected to God, who is powerful and all-knowing. He alone can turn evil into good. Turn wrongs into right. Turn sickness into healing. Turn hopelessness into hope. Turn disparity into prosperity. Turn grief into joy.

You might be in a pit in your own life right now. You might be dealing with a loved one's rejection. You might be battling despair and depression. You might be hurting. You might feel misunderstood. Your might believe your dreams have been deferred. You might be disappointed. But you need to grab hold of the fact that God has plans for you. "For I know the plans I have for you," declares the LORD, "plans to prosper you and not to harm you, plans to give you hope and a future" (Jer. 29:11).

Trouble will come for a season. Life will challenge you. When that happens, you must trust God's plan for your life. When you are focused on the will of God and when your faith is steady, something on the inside will assure you that God will turn it around. Good is promised to you, so you must declare and decree, "I know God will turn it around for my good."

God is going to turn your pit into an opportunity for you to witness His power.

When you understand that we live in a world where evil does exist, but the God you serve in faith can turn anything around for your good, then you can move through life with the blessed assurance that all will be well.

It doesn't matter what it looks like, feels like, or seems like. It doesn't matter what you hear in the boardroom, from the newsroom, or in your bedroom—don't give up on God. He will turn everything around for your good. He'll turn your children around. He'll turn your relationship around. He'll turn your spouse around. He'll turn your finances around. He'll turn your business around. He'll turn your job situation around. He'll turn your health around. He'll turn everything around for your good.

SPIRITUAL SOLUTIONS

1. Act on your dreams. What things has God spoken to you that you have yet to act on? What is keeping you from being faithful, focused, and fearless enough to pursue the dreams God has given to you?

_____

_____

_____

_____

_____

2. Put your fear in perspective. No matter what the world says, your future is secure in God. So even if you lose your home or job, God will turn it around for your good. Edify yourself by writing the ways God has protected you in the past.

_____

_____

_____

_____

_____

3. You are coming out of it. What have you been waiting for God to release you from? What will you do when God opens the gates and releases you into your purpose? Are you ready?

_____

_____

_____

_____

4. There is power in the pit. Do you feel like you're in life's pit? Look up and look over your life. List the ways God has brought you out in the past, so that you can remind yourself that He will do it again in the future.

_____

_____

_____

_____

_____

5. Declare God's goodness in your life. If you are facing a problem that is causing your faith to be diminished, now is the time to boldly declare and decree in faith, with confidence and conviction, "I know that God can and will turn this situation around for me and for my good." Now that you declared your faith restored, what are you going to do differently?

_____

_____

_____

_____

_____

Lesson 4

SUBMIT TO GOD'S WILL
FOR YOUR LIFE

AVE YOU EVER been in a battle against yourself? Have you ever experienced your flesh warring against your spirit? Seriously, have there been times when you really want to do the right thing, say the right thing, and act the right way—but you still do wrong?

There have been times in my own life when I struggled to stay on the straight and narrow path, and remain in the will of God. I, too, have had trouble being faithful, true, and consistent with the things of God. At one time or another, every one of God's children has struggled to do the Godly and righteous thing. Even Jesus, our Savior, the Son of God, our Redeemer, had to struggle with His purpose. In His heart, soul, and mind, Jesus struggled with His imminent destiny.

While He was in the Garden of Gethsemane at the Mount of Olives, Jesus was facing a struggle between His spirit and His flesh. After three years of ministering, healing, delivering, and teaching, Jesus' ultimate purpose was on the horizon. His ultimate purpose was near and Jesus struggled with it. Consider Jesus' experience in the Garden of Gethsemane as you face your own dilemmas and struggles. He must have asked Himself:

- Should I go and endure the suffering, the ridicule, the shame, the pain, the beating, and death on the cross—or should I avoid it?
- Should I get the nails hammered into my hands and my feet?
- Should I allow the crown of thorns to be crushed upon my

brow?

- Should I let the soldier pierce me in the side?

Jesus was human, and He was divine. It was His humanness, His flesh, that was questioning His purpose. His experience acknowledges the fight within that we all encounter, whether we are saved or not. But Jesus knew where to go to get assurance and confirmation; He went to His Father in prayer. When you find yourself in a war with yourself, or at a spiritual crossroad, do as Jesus did—turn to the one and only true and living God.

Jesus withdrew from His disciples, knelt down, and prayed alone. When you are really going through difficult times in life, you will hear Jesus saying, "Let's go to a quiet place and pray." When you are really going through and you need the Lord to work it out, do not waste time reaching for your cell phone, flipping it open, scrolling down, and calling your friends. There are some things in life that only God can do for you.

Instead of your friend's voice, you need the voice of God to tell you what you need, and to assure you and instruct you in the things of life. It doesn't matter what you think or what you want, or what others think or want.

When life presents you with a heart-wrenching, agonizing moment, get on your knees and pray.

God is in the midst and He is attuned to your prayers when you are humble and vulnerable. In your weakest moments, God will present you with opportunity to seek His face while He may be found.

Jesus prayed with honesty and sincerity. He openly told His Father how He felt. Imagine how He must have felt. He was only thirty-three years old; He was not ready to go. Jesus prayed, "Father, if You are willing, take this cup from me." But His love for God, His Father, and His desire to do God's will superseded His own temporary will and desire. Jesus then said, "Yet not my will, but yours be done" (Luke 22:42).

Jesus, on His knees in the garden on that day more than two thousand years ago, agonized over the decision to stay in the will of God. Jesus, knowing that in the Garden of Gethsemane, up ahead was the cross on Golgotha Hill. Jesus, in prayer and solitude, with His own power, gave up His will to the will of God. Jesus yielded in perfect obedience to the will of God.

When God is calling you to a higher and deeper place in Him, it is not unusual for you to respond out of your opinions, your flesh, your judgments, or the recommendations of others. But you must seek to mature in the things of God. You must seek God's face. Ask God what He wants you to do. Then be prepared to walk by faith and not by sight.

God is calling you develop a steady, consistent prayer life.

An angel appeared in the midst of Jesus' agony to strengthen, encourage, and support Him. Likewise, when you're in the midst of life's troubles and you seek God, he'll send you what you need until your change comes. He'll send a confirmation, a word of encouragement. He'll show you a sign. God will give you what you need to hang on in there until the breakthrough.

When you are in the will of God, He will send you what you need.

Jesus prayed so earnestly that His sweat was like drops of blood. Yet He still surrendered His will to God's will. He reached deeper within His soul in prayer, and He then yielded completely to God's will, and He stood up. He was ready to face His arrest and fulfill His purpose. He was ready to be humiliated, ridiculed, and spat upon. He was ready to be nailed to the cross and pierced in His side. Jesus was ready to take on our sins and die a terrible death, because He knew that resurrection was on the other side. He knew He was headed toward victory.

Jesus was the only begotten Son of God, and He was not exempt from problems. Why should it be any different for you? You are not exempt from struggles, difficulties, or dilemmas. But because of the Christ in you, even though you suffer sometimes, even though you may struggle sometimes, even though you may cry sometimes, you can rest assured that your victory is near. There is a victory day in Jesus Christ. There is a resurrection day. When your day of resurrection comes, you will realize that what seemed so difficult is no longer difficult. What seemed devastating is no longer devastating. What was unbearable is now bearable. What seemed was dead is now alive. Jesus Christ got up on the third day with all power. The enemy was defeated.

When you find yourself dealing with dilemmas, devastating situations, or other difficulties in life, know that Jesus has the power to fix it. Remember that Jesus has the power to do exceedingly and abundantly, above all you could ever think of or imagine. No weapon on this earth that is formed against you can prosper. Jesus paid it all on the cross for you. Now you must be willing to submit your will to God's will for your life.

I have not written what I think to be true; I wrote what I know to be true. I know that God will perform these things in your life, because He has done it for me in my life. Once I yielded my will to God's will, God blessed me. It's not a one-shot deal—God keeps blessing me over and over again; and He will do the same for you. I like to think of God's blessings as "every-time blessings" because:

- Every time I needed God, He moved.
- Every time I felt weak, God revealed His power.
- Every time I felt hopeless, God provided a way.
- Every time I was sick, God healed me.
- Every time I cried, He comforted me in the midnight hour.
- Every time I messed up, God forgave me.

God made a way out of no way for me, every single time I needed Him. When you submit to the will of God, He will bless you—it's as simple as that. Trust Him and submit. Not my will, but thy will be done. Not my stuff, by thy will be done. Not my opinion, but thy will be done. Not my judgment, but thy will be done.

SPIRITUAL SOLUTIONS

1. Ask Jesus first. When you have to make your next big decision, rather than call your best friend, ask Jesus. Then listen to His answer. Learn how to discern Jesus' "voice." He will answer you in various ways. Make sure you are attuned to Him. We often mistake Jesus with coincidence. Has anything ever just worked out for you? Write those instances down and look for Jesus in your responses.

_____

_____

_____

_____

_____

2. Find some time and space. Dedicate a time and space to talk to Jesus. If you don't have a designated prayer room in your house, don't fret. God can be found wherever you need Him to be. Jot down where and when you plan to spend some time with Him.

_____

_____

_____

_____

3. Watch what you say. Reflect back over the last storm you had to face. What did you say about it? Did you describe your situation as "overwhelming?" Did you tell yourself and others how stressed out you were? It's time to define a new vocabulary. Write five statements that you can use to empower yourself to make the right choice at your next crossroad in life.

_____

_____

_____

_____

_____

4. Don't look for an escape. None of us are exempt from life's problems, concerns, or issues. The good news is as long as you have Jesus, you don't need an escape hatch. Jesus gives you what you need to get through the situation and get on the other side. Write down five things God has brought you through in the last few months.

_____

_____

_____

_____

_____

5. Trust God in the process. Be willing to rest in the Lord in faith. Remember that God can instantly turn things around for you, or He may choose to do it over time. What diminishes your faith and trust in the Lord when you find yourself having to wait for God to move on your behalf?

_____

_____

_____

_____

_____

Lesson 5

Remember God's Promises

GOD TITLED THIS book *Faithful, Focused, and Fearless* for a reason. The order of the words themselves is important. The words represent a growth process—you can't be one thing without the other. In order to live fearless, you must be focused. In order to live focused, so that you can eventually live fearless, you must be faithful. It's a process.

The Bible is full of examples of people who were faithful. For example, Abraham's story has always strengthened my faith. His faith was exceedingly great. He was willing to do anything and everything that God asked of him, no matter what the personal cost.

In Genesis 22, God tests Abraham by telling him to sacrifice his only son, Isaac. Can you imagine being asked to sacrifice your child? Yet Abraham fully trusted God and was prepared to do what was required of him. He did not complain; he did not question God; he did not argue. Abraham prepared the altar to do God's will and sacrifice his beloved son. As he raised the knife in the air, an angel of the Lord stepped in and stopped Abraham from sacrificing his son. The angel said, "Do not do anything to him. Now I know that you fear God, because you have not withheld from me your son, your only son" (Gen. 22:12). God stepped in at the nick of time, not a moment too late, nor a moment too soon. Has God ever stepped into a situation that was testing your faith and instantly turned things around for you?

Abraham noticed a ram caught in a thicket by its horns. He took the ram and offered it up for a burnt offering instead of his son. Abraham called the place "The Lord Will Provide." I encourage you to take a lesson from Abraham. When God makes provision in your life, give Him His due. How often have you ever thought something happened for you, just at the right moment, by coincidence? It was no coincide—it was God. The ram was not in the bush by coincidence. God put it there to make a way for Abraham, and He has put a ram in the bush for you, too.

Not only did God spare his son's life, and make provision for him, He blessed Abraham beyond measure for his obedience. "I swear by myself, declares the Lord, that because you have done this and have not withheld your son, your only son, I will surely bless you and make your descendants as numerous as the stars in the sky and as the sand on the seashore. Your descendants will take possession of the cities of their enemies, and through your offspring all nations on earth will be blessed, because you have obeyed me" (Gen. 22:16–18). When you are obedient, God will bless you beyond all that you could ever think or imagine.

Abraham did not develop his deep abiding trust in God overnight. To truly understand how God moved in Abraham's life, I need to take you back to the beginning of his life, back before he received God's blessing.

In Genesis 12, God told Abraham, then called Abram, to leave his family, his father's house, and his comfortable familiar life, and go to a land that God would eventually show him. But, God also makes him a promise. God promises Abram that He will make a great nation through him. God also promises Abram that He would bless those who bless him and curse those who cursed him. God promises Abram that all the families of the earth, and that includes you and me, will be blessed. Abram was obedient, when the Lord spoke, he obeyed and he departed.

When God makes a promise to you, He keeps it.

When Abram starts his journey from Horan, he is seventy-five years old. With him are his wife Sarai, Lot, his brother's son, and all of his earthly possessions. (Just because God told you to go, don't assume that the journey will be easy.) The Bible says that when they got to the land of Canaan, they found it occupied by the Canaanites. But the Lord appeared again and made another promise to Abram, that "To your descendants I will give you this land." Abram continued on his journey stopping at place with Bethel on the west and Ai on the east, where he pitched a tent and built an altar. Then he traveled on toward the Negev. He eventually arrived in Egypt because there was a famine in the land.

Here's where things get interesting: Sarai was a beautiful woman, and Pharaoh was captivated by her beauty. Fearing for his life, Abram tells Sarai to tell Pharaoh that she is his sister, not his wife. Abram ends up being blessed with "sheep and cattle, male and female donkeys, menservants and maidservants, and camels."

Don't let a lie block your blessings—
anything you gain by lying will not last.

God was not pleased, and He sent a plague upon Pharaoh and his household. When Pharaoh discovers that the plagues occurred because of the lie, he banishes Abram, Sarai, and all who were with him (plus the servants and all of the livestock Pharaoh had given Abram), from Egypt. Abram returned to the Negev and eventually settled in the land between Bethel and Ai, where he had previously built an altar. He built another alter and called on the name of the Lord again.

Abram's lie continued to wreak havoc in his life even after he'd been banished from Egypt. Strife emerged between Abram's and Lot's men, because the land where they had temporarily settled could not support the massive amount of livestock. So, Lot and Abram go their separate ways. Lot chose the plain of Jordan, and pitched his tent near Sodom; whereas Abram chose to dwell in the land of Canaan.

Here's what I love about God, even after the lie, and after

Lot left him, the Bible says, God continued to make promises to Abram, "Lift up your eyes from where you are and look north and south, east and west. All the land that you see I will give to you and your offspring forever. I will make your offspring like the dust of the earth, so that if anyone could count the dust, then your offspring could be counted. Go, walk through the length and breadth of the land, for I am giving it to you" (Gen. 13:14–17).

When God makes an investment in you,
no matter what you do to mess things
up, God will reposition you for success.

Lot becomes entangled in a war between kings, and as a result, he and all of his possessions are taken captive. Abram gathers an army of 318 men, and they rescue Lot and retrieve his possessions. When the king of Sodom offers to make him rich, this time Abram knows better, "I have raised my hand to the LORD, God Most High, Creator of heaven and earth, and have taken an oath that I will accept nothing belonging to you, not even a thread or the thong of a sandal, so that you will never be able to say, 'I made Abram rich'" (Gen. 14:22–23). Do you see the difference in Abram? Part of becoming a faithful, focused, and fearless woman is learning from your past mistakes and making a commitment to God not to repeat the same mistakes over and over again.

In Genesis 15:1, God assures Abram's future success, telling him, "Do not be afraid, Abram. I am your shield, your very great reward." Although I believe Abram was grateful for God's protection, he wanted something more from the Lord; Abram wanted an heir, who was born of his own loins. And here is where the ultimate blessing begins to unfold. God promised to give Abram, not only an heir, but He tells Abram that his descendants will outnumber the stars in the heavens.

But you know how the story goes. Sarai suggested to Abram that he impregnate her maidservant Hagar. So, at eighty-six years old, Abram fathers Ishmael. But while she was pregnant, Hagar began to despise Sarai. I cannot stress enough the fact that when you decide to go against God's will, even though your intentions may be right, your plan will never work if it goes against God's will for your life.

When Abram is ninety-nine years old, the Lord appears to him again, and despite everything that has happened in the past thirteen years, God reconfirms His covenant with Abram. The Bible says that Abram fell on his face. It is here, that God touches Abram deep within and transitions him from one level of faith to a deeper level of faith. It is here that Abram hears God differently and receives God's promise to him in a place where he had not experienced God before. It is here the promise in the covenant is re-established.

It is here that the Lord changes Abram's name to Abraham, and establishes the promise in the covenant with the reiteration that Abraham shall be a father of all nations. God tells Abraham that his wife's name shall no longer be Sarai, but shall be changed to Sarah, and she will have a son, and she will be the mother of nations. Sarah, who was way past childbearing age, laughed at the thought that she would bear a son. Sometimes, things do appear to be impossible, but with God, all things are possible—Isaac was born to ninety-nine-year-old Sarah and one hundred-year-old Abraham.

You are never too old, nor is it ever too late to receive God's blessings.

After all Abraham and Sarah had gone through, from the time they left his father's house, God's blessings were starting to unfold in Abraham's life. Then, God tests Abraham's faith by asking him to sacrifice his and Sarah's long-awaited son. It was the ultimate test of faith; and Abraham was willing to do it without hesitation. But then God stepped in; Abraham looked up, and he saw his provision—God had given him a ram in the bush. Here's the thing I need you to understand: Abraham never doubted.

Take a lesson from Abraham and trust God's Word before:

- your promotion is announced
- a financial breakthrough hits your bank account
- your healing takes place
- you meet your spouse
- your spouse gets saved
- your marriage is restored
- your wayward child comes home and get saved
- the legal matter is resolved
- the depression is lifted
- you start looking for your new house

Speak it in faith, trust that the Lord will work it out for you, and believe it shall be so. For faith is the substance of things hoped for, and the evidence of things not seen. In fact, faith negates what we see in the natural. No matter what you're going through, you must trust God's promises in your life and hold on to His Word.

Just like God intervened in the nick of time for Abraham, the Lord will intervene for you also. Just like Abraham, you must be willing to always put God first and keep focused on the promise. You must never allow anyone or anything to be above God in your life or to make you question the veracity of God's promises to you.

God blessed Abraham and Sarah. He gave them the desires of their heart, and He fulfilled His promise because God saw that Abraham had his priorities in order, and he had an unshakable faith.

Look up and see God's provision in your own life. That thing you've been praying for, that thing you have been waiting for—look up and there it shall be. When you look up, the check you've been waiting for will arrive in the mail. When you look up, your promotion and raise will be announced. When you look up, your estranged child will be knocking at your front door. Whatever you are in need of, when you look up, you will see God's provision. He has the resources to provide everything you need. I know this is true because God has provided for me. I've been hungry, homeless, unemployed, sick, and lonely, but God worked it out. I am a living witness that God will do more than you could ever think or imagine when you look up. The Lord will work it out for you too. Just trust Him—try Him, depend on Him, and lean on Him. God will work it out. Stop worrying and start believing. If He did it before, He'll do it again.

The remarkable thing about Abraham's blessing is that it was generational; but it occurred thousands of years ago. I know it's hard for you to apply what happened way back then, when the situation you're facing is happening in the here and now. So, I want to share my generational blessing testimony with you to encourage you today. My grandmother had a sixth-grade education, and she raised seven children. My mother was next to the youngest. She was the first to go to college, a historical black college in Austin, Texas. She didn't finish, but years later, she had a daughter.

I grew up in Cambridge, went to elementary school, then on to Cambridge High Latin. I was one of the few black students who was a college prep student; yet, because I was one of the few black students, I never saw a counselor. No one in that school helped me decide what my next step after high school should be. During my sophomore year, I scored the highest grade on the English departmental exam. I didn't know how well I'd done until a brand new teacher took me outside of the classroom and whispered my accomplishment to me and admonished me not to disclose the information to anyone.

After I graduated, I attended a career and finishing school. After that, I got a job working for the Cambridge Redevelopment Authority, which was a federally funded organization. (They were attempting to diversify the workplace.) But the Holy Spirit kept on churning in my spirit, and the Lord said to me, "Go back to school. You can go to Brandeis University or Boston University."

I ended up getting a job at Boston University in the Martin Luther King Center. Less than a year later, the director told me about a federal program that recruited African-American students to attend Boston University. One of the twenty-one students who were enrolled in the program had dropped out. He asked me if I was still interested in attending Boston University.

He told me to go and see the admissions officer. I prayed as I walked to his office. He asked me to tell him about myself. I told him everything and he asked about my grades. I replied, "They were good." All of this occurred late Friday afternoon. I didn't take the trolley that day. Instead, I walked home from Boston to Cambridge praying to the Lord. "God, You will work it out. God, I know You will. I know You can work it out."

When I arrived at work on Monday morning, the director told me to go down and see the admissions officer again. I walked to his office, where he handed me my admissions letter to Boston University, without a transcript or SAT scores. It was the culmination of the promise. My grandmother did not go to college. My mother started, but did not finish. I was the beginning of the promise being fulfilled. Today, my daughter, Candace, has a bachelor's degree from Hampton University and she's working on her master's at Howard University; and my son is a Morehouse graduate. God will work it out. There is nothing too hard for God when you trust and believe.

Spiritual Solutions

1. Don't be a Sarai; be a Sarah. You must be patient while you're waiting for your blessing to be manifested. Resist the temptation to "help" God in your situation. Trust that things will happen for you exactly when they are supposed to occur. Life is a journey and a process. Are you really willing to wait until your promise is birthed into reality? What constructive things will you do in the meantime?

_____

_____

_____

_____

_____

2. It is time for a flashback. Is there anything too hard for the Lord? Hasn't God made provisions for you in the past? It's easy to forget how much God has done for you when you are facing an impending crisis. Take a moment to reflect and write down the way God has come through for you. Start from the beginning.

_____

_____

_____

_____

_____

3. Trust that God is working it out. God is at work in your circumstances. It doesn't matter what area of your life is being impacted: your health, your employment status, your family, your finances, or your mind. You must develop an assurance deep down in your soul that God will work it out. God wants to work it out for you. What areas of your life are you trusting God to work out?

_____

_____

_____

_____

_____

4. Get your priorities straight. Once your priorities are straight, God will fulfill the promise He spoke to you and give you the very desires of your heart. Never allow others to be above God in your life. Not your spouse, not your children, not your job—God must come first. Write down how you are glorifying God in all things in your life. If you find you can't write anything down, you may need to realign your priorities.

_____

_____

_____

_____

_____

5. Do not taint your blessings. If you're tired of waiting for God to bless you with a spouse, and you've made the decision to pursue someone else's spouse, you must stop now. If you're being considered for a promotion at work because you unfairly discredited a colleague, you need to make it right. If you've just signed a loan for a house or a car that you know will end in financial disaster, you know you're out of sync. Get honest with yourself and with God. Any blessings that you gain by telling a lie, will not last. Make a pledge to yourself and God to make it right.

_____

_____

_____

_____

_____

Lesson 6

REFUSE TO GIVE UP

H AS LIFE EVER dealt you an unexpected, unwanted, unbelievable, undesirable circumstance? Have you ever
faced a problem that could easily wipe you out? There
are challenges in life that come up suddenly, like a storm. This
kind of a situation can shadow your faith. Do you know what
I mean? Is there anything going on in your life that has caused
you to respond, "I can't take it any longer; I can't deal with what
is happening to me; I'm not going to make it?"

If your answer is "yes," you need to know, that no matter what
it feels like, this is not the time to give up. Instead, it's time for you
to put your hand in God's hand and step through that doorway of
pain, and fully trust that even though all hell might be breaking
out in your life, the Lord has everything under control.

This is the time to strengthen your faith, encourage your soul,
assure your heart, and declare that God will get you on the other
side. You will have the victory. You will win the battle. You will
land on your feet. You will not lose your mind. You will make it.

Where you are is not where
you will always be.

God is calling you to a place in Christ Jesus where you will
be able to hold on until God shows up and takes you out of the
situation. It is a place of confidence and holy boldness in the resurrection power of Jesus, the Christ. It is faith at its best. You will
be able to face your problem in faith, without fear or defeat, fully
trusting God in the midst of your storm. You will rest in the faith.

You will have hope. Why? Because you will be expecting God to move on your behalf. You will know with conviction that where you are is not where you will always be.

During times like these, you will learn how to reach out to Jesus to encourage your soul; and you will fully understand that the God of your salvation will come through for you in this time of trouble.

David is a perfect example of someone who fully believed in God's protective power. In Psalm 27:1–6, David finds himself in the midst of trouble. But notice, he is not afraid, because he knew where his help came from. It's comforting to know that when you are in trouble, the Lord will hide you in His pavilion, in the secret of His tabernacle. He will set you safely upon a rock.

But I want you to notice the shift in David's perspective in verse 7. He shifts from a position of trust and faith to a posture of lamenting and petitioning God to help him. He goes from a position of confident assurance because of how God has brought him out of trouble in the past, to one of sorrow and fear regarding his current troubles.

I'm sure you know what David was going through. Have you ever been delivered from one problem, only to have a new problem arise in your life? If you are not careful, your faith in God can get weak. But as a fearless child of God, it's time for you to boldly walk through the door of the problem. Sit in the middle of it, look it in the eye in the faith, and seek God's face and seek God's favor, for this is not the time to give up.

> *Your faith walk must be consistent.*
> *Don't praise God for bringing you*
> *out one day, and then wonder if*
> *He can bring you out the next.*

David needed God to work it out in his present situation, yet he was a little afraid. God wants you to know that He will handle whatever is going on in your life right now—God will handle your present stuff. Things can happen so fast; life can change so quickly. You need to know that the God you serve will never forsake you. When the unwanted, unexpected, unbearable things occur in your life, the enemy can have a field day with you.

In verse 10, David ponders the possibility of being forsaken by his parents. While he is considering this worst-case scenario, his faith in the Lord begins to reactivate. On life's journey, sometimes the people who are the closest and the dearest to you can disappoint you. You expect certain things from certain people. When you don't get the response you were expecting it can throw you for a loop. Or the people closest to you may be located elsewhere, or they may be disabled and unable to help in the time of need, or they have gone home to be with the Lord.

In other words, there may come a time when you feel helpless and alone. But if you are faithful, focused, and fearless, you know that the Lord will help you. The Lord Jesus Christ is our helper. The Lord will take you up in Him, and He will rock you in His arms until the change comes.

David asked the Lord for specific help. He asked God to teach, lead, and deliver him. What more can you ask of the Lord? Especially now, in these turbulent times, you must not lean not on your own understanding; but in all your ways, acknowledge God, and ask Him to teach, lead, and deliver you.

Like David, you must constantly pray for divine guidance as you journey through this life. You might be facing problems and difficulties, and you might feel like giving up and throwing in the towel. This is not the time to quit.

Now is the time to put your faith and trust in the Lord Jesus Christ. Seek His face. Let the Lord guide you. Depend and rely upon Him. There is always hope in the Lord. This is not the time to give up. Although David starts out faithful, then moves to sorrow, he ends with his faith restored, when he states, "I am still confident of this: I will see the goodness of the Lord in the land of the living. Wait for the Lord; be strong and take heart and wait for the Lord" (Ps. 27:13–14).

David realized that he could confidently expect God to show

up the next time he was faced with a problem, concern, or hurt. So, although you may be in the middle of some mess, fainting is not an option. You've got to dig deep and hold on.

As you sit there staring at your pink slip, or watching the movers clear out your dream home and repossess your dream car, or realizing that your spouse is not coming back, don't faint. This is not the time to give up. This is the time to believe and see the goodness of the Lord in the land of the living.

Look around and see God—see your layoff as a time to start your business and use your God-given talents to do something that you're truly passionate about, see your foreclosure as an opportunity to budget and live within your means and not to someone else's standards, see your new marital status as an opportunity to rediscover some element of yourself that was buried under a failed marriage. See it in the spirit realm. Just imagine how the Lord will work it out for you. Look and see that everything is really going be all right. When the Lord is your shepherd, goodness and mercy shall follow you all the days of your life.

You must believe that whatever trouble you are facing today, God is using it as an opportunity to awaken something on the inside of you. Keep on moving forward until your change comes.

You should know deep down in your sanctified soul that God will surely come.

You must wait on the Lord and be of good courage. And He shall strengthen thy heart. Wait, in faith, for the Lord to work it out. There is nothing that is too hard for God. God can give you a peace that passes all understanding. So even if the doctors says it's cancer, or the bank says you have no funds available, or your credit score plummets—you will have peace. Bad news will not destroy you. You will not worry; you will not fret. You will stand strong in the Lord. Wait on the lord for everything you need. Wait for:

- your promotion and a raise
- your healing
- your broken heart to be restored

Wait in the faith for the Lord to do what He said He would do for you, and be of good courage. The wait in faith is a part of the journey. The wait in faith is a guarantee of the victory. The Lord Jesus Christ, on that old, rugged cross, could have avoided the agony and gone on to glory; but instead He hung there, suffered, bled, and died. He went into the grave, and on the third day, got up with all power.

This is not the time to give up. This is not the time to let go. They that wait upon the Lord shall renew their strength. They shall mount up as wings with an eagle. They shall run and not get weary. They shall walk and not faint.

The Lord will see you through, bring you out, and make a way for you to move on to something better. He will deliver you and set you free. This is not the time for you to question God. This is not the time for you to buckle in the faith. This is the time for you to stand boldly in your situation, activate your faith, and claim your victory even before you see it.

We all have problems and difficulties. I guarantee you that your journey of faith will be marked by troubles and concerns. But God can, will, and wants to get you through it. This is not the time to give up, not now, not ever.

SPIRITUAL SOLUTIONS

1. Refuse to give up. Resolve to keep your faith as your step into the pat of your pain. This is not the time for you to give up. Instead, write your plan for how you will reach for God and place and trust in God. Recall how you used to respond to adversity and envision how you will respond now as a faithful, focused, and fearless child of God.

_____

_____

_____

_____

_____

2. Let the enemy know you are no longer bound by fear. When you are in the heat of the situation, you must put the enemy on notice that you are not afraid of him. Write a declaration of your faith. You will be able to refer to it when things get hard. Do you believe Jesus will see you through this? Do you trust Him? Do you truly believe that He will never leave or forsake you? Write a few statements that you can use to fortify yourself in the face of your next problem.

_____

_____

_____

_____

_____

3. Ask like David. David asked the Lord to teach, lead, and deliver him through his troubles. Are you ready for God to teach, lead, and deliver you? If so, what specific areas in your life are you seeking God's help in? Has God already spoken to you about it?

_____

_____

_____

_____

_____

4. Flex your faith with your testimony. Sometimes you can encourage yourself when you're going through a painful situation simply by giving your testimony to someone else. You don't have to wait until God carries you through and over your problem. You can claim victory in advance. Who will you tell about what God has done for you, and what will you tell them?

_____

_____

_____

_____

_____

5. This is not the time to give up. Your faith will keep you from fainting in times of trouble. As you journey through this life, like David, when you are faced with troubles, you need to remember that God is a present help. Here's your chance to write your own personal Psalm. Write your own prayer of praise and thanksgiving. Use it to encourage yourself when you feel weak in the faith.

_____

_____

_____

_____

_____

Lesson 7

TRUST GOD TO
TAKE CARE OF YOU

A T SOME POINT in your life you will find yourself distressed, depressed, and full of despair. However, once
you begin to trust and believe that God will take care
of you, you can rest in the blessed assurance that your present
trouble will not last. You will know beyond a shadow of a doubt,
that God will step into the midst of your troubles and all will be
well again.

It amazes me how, in spite of our sins and sinful natures and
our wrongdoings, God still takes care of you and me. God still
blesses us. God still keeps and provides for us. Even though we
have not always done the right thing in the sight of God, He has
kept us in the palm of us His hand.

Think about it: God's love for you is so profound that He sent
His only begotten Son through forty-two generations to die for
your sins. He commissioned him to heal the sick, raise the dead,
cast out demons, and to preach and teach, all so that you could
live an abundant life. Jesus paid it all for you on the Cross. He
suffered for your salvation. He rose to ensure your victory.

On this journey through life, you can be sure trouble will
come. For example, your son or daughter who you raised in the
church has discovered the street and the allure of nightlife. They
are hanging out with the wrong crowd, and you fear that they
are living a life contrary to what you had planned for them. You
feel like you no longer have a say in the direction their lives are

headed. You've been praying for God to intervene, but you're beginning to wonder if God heard your prayers.

You need to know that because you did what the Word of God said, and trained up your child in the way he or she should go, they will find their way back. Just like the prodigal son, they will return to the God of their salvation.

You may be battling demons in your marriage, your relationship, your workplace, your business, or in your health. You may not be convinced that God will come through for you. There are some things that occur in life that can shake the very core of your being. The death of a loved one, divorce, job loss, foreclosure—these things can be devastating. Even if you've been saved for twenty years, the heaviness of grief can overwhelm you and make you feel like you are not going to make it. But you can find comfort in Jesus.

God will send the Holy Spirit to comfort you. I'm talking about supernatural comfort. It's the kind of comfort that allows you to know that despite the fact that all hell is breaking loose around you; your joy will be restored. The scriptures become real and authentic in your heart, and God gives you a peace that passes all understanding.

> *You might cry yourself to sleep,*
> *but if you believe, you will wake*
> *up with your joy restored.*

In the midst of your troubles and concerns, if you are walking through life with an authentic, heartfelt faith and trust in God, He will take care of you. If you are not, it's not too late to start. God will take care of you if you would just try Jesus and embrace Him in faith. When you do, there will be a place within you that speaks to you, that settles you, and that assures you that no matter what it seems like, God will work it out. You will realize the truth in Psalm 23, that as you walk through the valley of the shadow of death, the Lord is your Shepherd and you shall not want. You shall fear no evil, for His rod and His staff will comfort you. You will know what so many saints of God already know and believe to be true—the Lord is your refuge and your fortress in the time of trouble.

As David walked through his journey of life he penned Psalm 138 to thank God for answering his prayers. As David thinks of his past and looks toward his future, he affirms his faith because he knew that God preserved his life. He knew that God had protected him, provided for him, and sustained him in spite of himself.

David realized trouble is a constant fact of life. It comes over and over again; but like David, you should be assured that God will take care of you. In Psalm 38:7 David writes, "Though I walk in the midst of trouble, you preserve my life; you stretch out your hand against the anger of my foes, with your right hand you save me." In other words, in times of trouble, God will give you the strength to endure.

In this life you will constantly face new realities.

I think people believe that because I am a pastor, I don't have to face my fair share of trouble. Let me assure you, not one of us walks through life without trouble. We all experience trouble because of the introduction of sin at the beginning of time. Trouble and trials are a part of life:

- Our bodies get sick.
- We disagree with friends and loved ones.
- Death knocks at our door.
- We face disappointments.
- Corruption and crime occurs in our communities.

But through it all God will take care of you. God will support you. God will carry you. God will be your refuge and your strength. God is an all-sufficient God at all times. There is nothing too hard for God.

You will not lose your mind because although God sits high,

He looks low. He is willing to take care of you and your troubles if you will just let go and trust Him. There is no enemy from which God cannot deliver you. There is no trial that He cannot overcome. There is no danger from which He cannot rescue you. In the fiery furnaces of life, He will be there to keep you. In the lion's dens of life He is with you. He will lock the jaws of any predator that is trying to devour you. He is a wonder-working God.

> ### *It is comforting to know that in the midst of trouble, God will take care of you.*

As Christians we never walk alone. As the Bible says, we are troubled on every side, yet not distressed. We are perplexed, but not in despair. Persecuted, but not forsaken. Cast down but not destroyed. For our light affliction is just for a moment. Therefore, don't focus your attention on things that are temporal, like trouble, focus on the eternal.

When you find yourself in trouble, look back over your life and remember how God took care of you before. Fortify yourself and remember that if God did it before, He will do it again. Know that whatever comes your way God has given you the capacity to withstand it. Know that in your trouble, God will perfect that which concerns you.

He who began a good work in you will complete it. God will complete everything that He promised you. God will complete that which He spoke down in your soul. When you are in trouble, you ought to know, as David knew, that the Lord will be your refuge and a very present help in times of trouble. I encourage you to place your problem in God's capable hands, and rest assured that the Lord shall keep you.

The Lord shall preserve, protect, and provide for you. The Lord shall do just what He said He'd do. God will keep working on your behalf, until that which He started and that which He has promised is complete.

As you face realities of the current economic situation and its impacts on your personal finances, you might wonder if God really will intervene in your situation. You might think that with everything that is occurring in the world today, your problem is too small to catch God's attention. God told me to tell you, He can do anything but fail. God cares for each and every one of us. He can end wars and rectify your bank account in an instant—trust and believe! God plans for your prosperity.

In Christ Jesus you are saved by grace. Jesus is your keeper. When you embrace God's deep and abiding love, you will live a life of confidence, not in yourself, but in God Almighty. As you walk in the midst of life and the unavoidable reality that troubles will come and go, you can rest in the faith that no matter what it looks like, and no matter what it feels like, there is a God who can do anything but fail. God will take care of you.

The older I get, the more I realize that the words to the hymn, *God Will Take Care of You*, really are true. It has been a difficult year for all of us, myself included. That's one of the wonderful things about writing this book. As God spoke through me, to share these words with you, I, too, became more faithful, focused, and fearless. This book has renewed my own testimony. I was reminded of God's healing power in my life on several occasions.

So although I may not know what troubles are lurking around your life, I do know that God will work it out for you if you would just put your faith in Him. Troubles will come and troubles will go, but there is a God that can do anything but fail.

SPIRITUAL SOLUTIONS

1. Ask for the assurance you need. Did you realize that you can go to God and ask Him to help you? So often believers think that they have to go through their pastors or other church leaders to get a prayer through to God. Here's your chance to write your own petition. God's ear is always inclined to you. After you write it out, tell God what you need Him to do for you.

_____

_____

_____

_____

_____

2. Put your faith in God. Far too often, we suffer needlessly because we insist on relying on our own strength and intellect to resolve our problems. Don't you realize that God is waiting to perfect that which concerneth you? He's waiting for you to put your faith in Him. Think about the things you've been trying to accomplish on your own power and write a list of the things you will relinquish to God today. Then, put your faith in Him to do what you've asked Him to do.

_____

_____

_____

_____

_____

3. Testify to yourself. Many churches have a time in the program, where congregants can stand up and give a personal testimony. I don't know the dynamics of your church home (and I'm sincerely praying that you have a church home, and if not I'm praying you'll find one soon), but if you can't testify in church, testify in the mirror. Write your testimony and then read it aloud to

yourself, as a reminder of all of the marvelous and miraculous things that God has done for you.

———————————————————————
———————————————————————
———————————————————————
———————————————————————
———————————————————————

4. Write your laundry list. God has been good to all of us in spite of ourselves. If we all would sit long enough and let the Lord bring to our remembrance our laundry list of what we have done to grieve the heart of God. This year alone we all would want to go somewhere and hide.

———————————————————————
———————————————————————
———————————————————————
———————————————————————
———————————————————————

5. Reflect on God's care. Take a moment to reflect on all of the ways in which God has taken care of you. Make a list of all the times God has made a "way out" of no way in your life. Get on your knees and thank God for all that He has done and for all that He is going to do in your life.

———————————————————————
———————————————————————
———————————————————————
———————————————————————
———————————————————————

Lesson 8

STAND STILL AND
SEE THE VICTORY

THERE IS A reality in all of our lives. We all experience and find ourselves dealing with life's battles. Some battles are the result of conflicting and opposing realities. You can experience battles internally and externally; but no matter what form they take, battles can leave you feeling hurt and discouraged. Some battles will be minor, temporary inconveniences that have little impact on your life.

But then there are those battles that linger and can wear you down, because the resolution of the conflict seems to be nowhere in sight. Consider the current economy, the lingering downturn, high unemployment numbers, and the uncertainty regarding the future. The suffering is wearing everyone down. We all want it to be over. It's this type of battle that will mess with your faith and cause you to question the majesty and the sovereignty of God.

The Lord wants to encourage and empower you in the midst of your particular battle, that particular battle that you have been waiting and praying to be resolved. God wants you to learn how to stand till in the battle and see the victory.

Life presents battles whether you want them or not. You will encounter battles in:

- your family
- your relationships
- your marriage
- your job

- your health
- your school

Sometimes you can do everything in your power to resolve your battle, and yet there is no victory in sight—that's where your faith must step in. The Lord wants you to give your battles, problems, and concerns to Him. Especially those battles that appear to be overwhelming, and those problems in which the odds seem to be stacked against you, and those concerns that make you feel like you're outnumbered ten to one.

When you feel like no one else cares what you are going through, know that God does.

You might be facing a battle on your job. Maybe you are not considered for the promotion. Instead, the person you trained gets the job. You might be facing a battle in your body. Your health is deteriorating and the doctors do not know why. Your might be facing a battle to find your purpose. Your future is unclear; you can't seem to find your niche, your passion, your purpose. You might be facing a spiritual battle. Your old stuff, old ways, old attitudes are rising up, and you are confused and weary, unhappy, and discontent.

God wants you to step up into a new place in Him. He wants you to exist in a faith place that requires you to make a conscious effort to change and a conscious effort to allow Him to speak to your soul and settle you in the midst of your battles, so that you can experience victory in all things. There is something wonderful happens on the inside when you are able to see and face your battles as God sees them.

Consider the familiar story of King Jehoshaphat and the people of Judah in 2 Chronicles 20 and how the Lord responded to King Jehoshaphat and the people of Judah during their very difficult times.

King Jehoshaphat was aware that the enemies of the people of Judah are coming. When he is first informed, the Bible says that King Jehoshaphat was fearful. When you are in the midst of a problem, fear can creep in and mess with your faith. When that happens, you need to remember what the Word says in 2 Timothy 1:7: "God hath not given us the spirit of fear; but of power, and of love, and of a sound mind" (KJV).

Like King Jehoshaphat, you must seek the Lord in times of distress. The king and the people of Judah gathered themselves and called on the Lord. The Bible declared that the king began a roll call to the Lord to remind himself what the Lord had done for His people in the past.

You see, sometimes in your battles you have to encourage yourself. You must reminisce and have a flashback of how good God has been to you in the past, recall how far He has brought you, recount miracles He has performed in your life, and re-examine how He brought you through so many unbelievable circumstances and situations in the past. Look back at how He intervened on your behalf even when you did not deserve it. You know you should have gotten caught in your mess; but God wiped the slate clean.

And like the king, when you are now faced with yet another battle and evil comes and sits on you, the king said we will stand because of who God is. In other words, in the journey of faith, when evil comes you need to recognize who God is. He is this great, wonderful, powerful, wonder-working miracle God that can and will do anything but fail. You must recognize and acknowledge this God, and believe in your heart, soul, and mind that there is none like Him.

> *Get specific with God. When you*
> *call on God for help, tell Him*
> *exactly what you're facing.*

King Jehoshaphat then cries out to the Lord about what the people are up against. That their enemies are coming for them to drive them out and take their possessions they inherited.

Know this, that in your battles in life, the evil one is always trying to take your stuff. He's always trying to take something that God gave you, promised to you, or blessed you with. The evil one is coming to try to kill, steal, and destroy. The evil one is coming for your blessings from the Lord. He's coming for:

- your family
- your children
- your marriage
- your health
- your job
- your finances
- your home
- your possessions
- your relationships
- your friendships
- your mind
- your emotions
- your peace
- your joy
- your prosperity

The enemy knows that he can attack you through the things and the people that matter to you most. The evil one is coming for anything that God has blessed you with because he wants you to leave God. He wants you to leave your church. He wants you to leave your loved ones.

Let me tell you what else he wants you to do. He wants you to curse like a sailor. He wants you to take drugs and drink, so that you'll end up an addict or an alcoholic. He wants you to change your lifestyle. He wants you to cut up and act a fool. Why? So that the Lord will no longer be glorified in your life. The enemy wants to wage war in your life and convince you that he will win, so that God will not be glorified in you.

But it's time for you to stop your pity party and serve notice to the enemy that his time is up. It's time for you to declare victory in the Lord. I know you're scared; but this battle has messed with your faith long enough. This battle that has caused your knees to buckle, your foundation to shift, and your resolve to weaken is no longer yours, it's the Lord's. Now stand still and see it as the Lord sees it and see victory.

King Jehoshaphat cried out to the Lord and asked Him to execute judgment upon his enemies. He felt powerless against such a great multitude and did not know what to do. Have you ever felt powerless and overwhelmed? You tried everything and to no avail.

But like King Jehoshaphat cried out to the Lord and said, in 2 Chronicles 20:12, "For we have no power to face this vast army that is attacking us. We do not know what to do, but our eyes are upon you," the Lord wants you to fix your eyes upon Him. Look to the hills for whence cometh your help because your help comes from the Lord.

The Bible said the men and the babies and the children and the wives stood before the Lord. It was then that the Spirit of the Lord came upon Jahaziel, the son of Zachariah, who said "This is what the LORD says to you: 'Do not be afraid or discouraged because of this vast army. For the battle is not yours, but God's'" (2 Chron. 20:16). His words were true then, and they are still true today.

In other words, what it appears to be and what you see and what it seems like and what it feels like do not matter. This battle that is threatening to wipe you out and overwhelm you; this battle that has lingered far too long; this battle that you have tried to fight and fix on your own; this battle that keeps you up all night wiping your tears; this battle that won't let you go, the one that drains you, the one that exhausts you; this battle is not yours—but the Lord's.

And now, the Lord is preparing you to come out of it. But there are some things you must do:

- Release your fear—let it go.
- Don't worry—God is in control.
- Stop fighting—this battle belongs to God.
- Realize where your help comes from—God has your back.

In 2 Chronicles 20:17, the Bible says, "Take up your positions; stand firm and see the deliverance the LORD will give you, O Judah and Jerusalem. Do not be afraid; do not be discouraged. Go out to face them tomorrow, and the LORD will be with you." In other words, you do not have to shrink because the enemy has you in a battle. You don't have to back up from anything or anybody or any situation.

In other words, activate your faith in a God who will not leave you or forsake you. Activate your faith and know greater is He that is in you, than He that is in the world. Activate your faith that with God nothing shall be impossible. Activate your faith and know that you are more than a conquerer through Him that loves you. Activate your faith and go not in defeat, but go in conviction and confidence knowing that in the Lord Jesus Christ victory is yours.

Stand still in the Lord and see the victory.

The Bible says once they got their marching orders, they fell down and worshiped the Lord. They praised and worshiped the Lord with a very loud voice before the battle, before the victory, before the blessing. When praises go up, blessings come down.

The Bible said the next morning they went to the enemies' camp. They marched together, the men and the women, the boys and the girls. And King Jehoshaphat said, "Listen to me, Judah and people of Jerusalem! Have faith in the LORD your God and you will be upheld; have faith in his prophets and you will be successful" (2 Chron. 20:20). And the Bible said the singers sang, and they worshiped unto the Lord. And while they sang, the Lord set up an ambush.

While the people of God were praising God, the Lord made the enemies get confused. The enemies who had collaborated together against the people of God ended up turning against each other and killing each other. Those who have collaborated against you behind closed doors, those enemies on your job who appear to be working against you, God is going to flip the script, and it is going to be in your favor.

The Bible says, in 2 Chronicles 20:24, that when the people of Judah came to the watchtower of the wilderness, instead of them being in a battle with the enemies, they were able to recoup the spoils of the enemies' camp. There were so many articles of value and equipment and gold and silver and clothing, they couldn't take it all. The Bible says it took three days for them to collect everything. After they gathered their blessings on the fourth day, they assembled in Valley of Beracah, the Valley of Blessings, and they returned to Jerusalem with joy.

When you are focused on the Lord and you have the Lord on your side, you will experience things differently. You will no longer look at life the same way. Your faith will enable you to experience and see things differently. You will be fearless because of what the Lord Jesus Christ did on that old, rugged Cross. You will be victorious because He suffered, bled, died, and rose up again with all power in His hands.

You will have the blessed assurance to know that what appears to be a losing battle, God can turn it into a victory. What appears to be the last, God can always make it the first. What appears to be lost, God can always gain it back. What appears to be sickness unto death, the Lord God can heal. What appears to be the end can be a new beginning. What appears to be the place of the worst of times can be flipped and end up being the best of times.

You will see that there is nothing too hard for God, when you are able to stand still and see your life being ordered by God. See your enemies become your footstools. See your setbacks become your comebacks. See your weakness become your strength. See your lack become your blessing. See your battles as the Lord sees them. In Christ only, you are able to see not in the natural but in the supernatural. You will be able to stand in the midst of the battle and see supernaturally in faith that God can do anything but fail. That God can turn it around. That God is able.

That God loves you like nobody else does. That God wants you to be blessed. That God can do exceedingly, abundantly, above all you can think or measure, that you are in a win-win situation in the Lord Jesus Christ.

You have been trying to fight life's battles in the natural. God told me to tell you to press in closer to Jesus, activate your faith, and see the victory in the name of Jesus. See your healing. See your prosperity. See your kids saved. See your marriage fixed. See your spouse back home. See God. Stand still. See what God can do. See the victory!

SPIRITUAL SOLUTIONS

1. Face your battles. There are some battles in life that we can easily resolve. But there are many battles we live through that we need the Lord's help. What battles have you been fighting and for how long? Do you believe that this battle is yours to fight or do your realize you would be more victorious if you take your hands off of it and give it to God? Will you?

_____

_____

_____

_____

_____

2. Reach for a faith place. Have you been fighting a long battle in which there seems no immediate resolution is in sight? If so, make a conscious effort to reach for a faith place in the Lord. Communicate with God as you would a trusted friend. Get specific with God. Go to a place in the Lord that settles your soul, even though the battle is raging, even though the problem may be mushrooming. Reach for that place that sees the battle as God sees it, and visualize the victory up ahead.

_____

_____

_____

_____

3. Trust that God will bless you. After they stood up to their enemies, it took three days for the people of Judah to collect their blessings. God's getting ready to bless you with so much that you will not be able to take it in all at once, but you've got to be willing to stand firm. What have you been shrinking away from?

What about your current circumstance intimidates you? Use this space to ask God to give you the strength to stand firm.

_____

_____

_____

_____

_____

4. Praise Him in advance. The people of Judah gave praise even before they got the victory. What are you praising while you wait for your victory? If you're worried, you're not praising. If you're scared, you're not praising. You don't have to be a gospel composer to write your own praise song. Write a few lines to encourage yourself and praise God in advance.

_____

_____

_____

_____

_____

5. Understand that life is a journey of faith. You won't always be strolling down Zipadeedoodah Lane. You will face trouble. The question is, what will you do when trouble comes? Where is your faith? In the battle, where do you stand? Who will you turn to? What will you do when trouble comes?

_____

_____

_____

_____

_____

Lesson 9

BE WILLING TO CHANGE

SOME OF US are deathly afraid of change, but change can be good. President Barack Obama ran his campaign primarily with the emphasis on the need for a change—a change in how the government was governing; a change in politics as usual; and, a change in how decisions were being made in the White House concerning the economy, education, health, and the war in Iraq.

During his campaign, he gave us a new, fresh perspective. He had in the faith, the audacity of hope. President Barack Obama possessed a steadiness and a resiliency, and he refused to crumble and compromise his platform of change while he was under incredible pressure and scrutiny.

It was obvious that he had something very strong, powerful, and clear on the inside that spoke to his conviction that he was the man to do the job and be the agent of change. His wife, Michelle Obama, would reiterate over and over again, who her husband was and how he was the one who was called to bring change to this country. No matter what his opponents tried to throw at him, he grew stronger, and he became more presidential.

The masses voted for him and his platform of change. The Obamas are a breath of fresh air. I believe Barack Obama was sent by God for such a time as this. As the first African-American President of the United States of America, he and his family are a shining example of God's ability to do the seemingly impossible.

You have seen what change can bring about. Now, the Lord

wants to speak a word of change to you, if you are willing to embrace the place within that you need to change.

At some point, everything must
change. Trust God in the change.

The Lord is challenging you to identify the area or areas you need to change and bring before the Lord so that you can truly be faithful, focused, and fearless. So, the first hurdle is admitting the need to change. It is saying to yourself and the Lord, "I need to change in this area of my life because this area has direct impact on who I am in the Lord." It is realizing that something is hindering your spiritual growth.

We often find ourselves spiritually stuck, and it's an easy way to point the finger outward and not inward to self and find yourself in a spiritual rut. When this happens you are unable to engage and connect with the Holy Spirit, who empowers you. You end up stuck in a place that prevents you from moving forward and embracing change. However, acknowledging and confessing that you need to change, opens the door for the Lord to work a miracle in you.

In his letters to the church in Corinth, Paul writes about serving the Lord and living and moving through life as a Christian. Paul was ever so conscious of being a servant of the Lord, as an apostle. As a Christian, he was ever so conscious of who he was in Christ Jesus, especially in light of his human sinful nature and the reality of his past as a persecutor on the road to Damascus.

Paul lived his life with a constant, consistent reality of who he was and who he was striving to be in Christ. His role and responsibility was ever before him and he lived his life out of that reality. He was forever reaching and unfolding to become the man God wanted him to be.

Paul discusses the temporary nature of life—the earth is a temporary dwelling place. After a while, your flesh will dissolve.

Everything that was going north, starts going south. That which houses our soul will give way.

Then Paul tells us about the new body, the spiritual body, which gives us what we need to strive and to adore God. Paul viewed eternity, the heavenly place, as a place within our bodies in the presence of the Lord in which we could be complete and whole in the Lord.

Therefore, as you live on Earth, you must move and strive toward your heavenly home within because you already have access to it. You can possess the Holy Spirit of God on earth. The Holy Spirit gives you the opportunity to have a taste of heaven. In other words, you don't need to be down here miserable, always looking for heaven. You need to embrace the reality that you can live and have a touch of heaven on earth.

As a Christian, you can enjoy a foretaste of the life of everlasting on Earth.

As you live in this world, you are not of this world. You are a citizen of two worlds—the natural and the spiritual. When you live your life with this reality, you can see God in your reality, and you will be able to see the greater glory of His works.

This does not mean that you should walk around with your head in the clouds. You must embrace the reality that there's good and evil. There's bad and good. You live in the context of who you are in Christ Jesus in this world. You must be aware of your surroundings as you seek and embrace the God of your salvation. You should live life differently because you are aware of God's hand moving on your behalf despite the reality of evil.

Now, with a kind of awareness and consciousness, you are also keenly aware that as a Christian, when the end comes and you are on your way to glory, you will be judged. Therefore, you must always be conscious of your conduct. You must live a life that is pleasing in God's sight. With this in mind, you should approach life consciously, embracing all that the Lord has for you on earth, with the understanding that at the end of your journey, you want God to be pleased with how you've lived.

> *The life you live on earth is your testing*
> *ground for your eternal home in heaven.*

I know this is deep stuff, but you must understand it. Even though there will be a time when you will stand in judgment, that does not mean you should be afraid. Rather than fear God's judgment, you need to revere His awesome power. Job 28:28 says, "The fear of the LORD, that is wisdom; and to depart from evil is understanding" (KJV). Therefore, it is wise to live your life in the context of who God is and the reality that you are going to be judged at the end of your life.

The following scriptures clarify what it means to fear or revere the Lord:

> What doth the LORD thy God require of thee; to
> fear the LORD thy God.
> —DEUTERONOMY 10:12, KJV
> By mercy and truth iniquity is purged: and by the
> fear of the Lord men depart from evil.
> —PROVERBS 16:6, KJV
> The fear of the Lord is clean, enduring for ever:
> the judgments of the Lord are true and righteous
> altogether.
> —PSALM 19:9, KJV

Therefore, as you revere, fear, and stand in awe of the Lord, you also desire to live a more righteous life. Paul lived his life motivated by a need to serve God. Paul was often viewed as crazy because he was sold out for the Lord. For example, in Acts 26:24, when Paul was on trial before king Agrippa, Festus interrupted Paul's testimony about the change that took place in his life on the road to Damascus, saying, "You are out of your mind, Paul!" he shouted. "Your great learning is driving you insane."

When you are sold out for Jesus and you stand boldly for the things of God, there will be those around you who will think you are a holy roller. They will try to convince you there is something wrong with you because you are trying to live the life that God has called you to live. When it comes down to it, it is all about living for Christ and being willing to yield and change. The Word of God is clear, "Therefore if any man be in Christ, he is a new creature: old things are passed away; behold, all things are become new" (2 Cor. 5:17, KJV).

In other words, you need to change. Change is good. To change means to make a radical difference in what you do. When it's radical you don't go back to it. When it's radical, you're determined to stick to the change. To change means to make a shift from one way to another way, to become different.

In other words, Paul is saying that in Christ there should be a radical change in our personal, private lives. It's one thing to look like you live holy in church, but what happens when you leave the sanctuary? Is your life consistent?

As a faithful, focused, and fearless child of God, you must release your hidden and commit to a new standard. If you're going to live for God, you must release your old ways and habits. In fact, your entire outlook on life must change. When Christ resides in you, He calls you to make a radical break from your old ways, and embrace the new: a new way of living, thinking, and interpreting life. The Lord wants you to be willing to let Him change some things on the inside, so that you can be new in Him. Old things, let them pass away and behold all things are becoming new. Choose to become a new creation in Christ, with new attitudes, new actions, and new ways of doing things.

> *Tell God the things you want Him*
> *to change in your life, and watch*
> *Him begin a new thing in you.*

It's time for you to stop drinking, fornicating, and smoking. It's time for you to stop procrastinating and being inconsistent. The lying and gossiping must stop. If you've been plagued by the demons of jealousy, gluttony, envy, or laziness ask the Lord to release you.

God is calling you forth. He wants you to admit that there are areas in your life that need to change, so you can receive what the Lord has for you. If you will allow the Lord deliver you and change you, He will bless you.

This walk with the Lord is not a stroll; it is a journey. It is an ongoing process of renewal. I was saved at twelve. I accepted Christ and joined the church. However, I was twenty-six years old before I had my transforming experience. I was living life, but I wasn't all that I felt that I needed to be in Christ Jesus.

You may know the Lord, but you're still out of place. You may very well know Him, but you've yet to be transformed by Him. I had a relationship with God, but I found myself wanting to go another level. I needed more. I needed something else. So I asked, "God, what do I need to do?" Because I knew Him, I knew His voice, but there was still another level, I needed to reach in Him.

The Lord told me "Go to St. Thomas and see your girlfriend, Cynthia. I want you to sit and be quiet with me." So, I went to St. Thomas. For six days I sat on the beach with my girlfriend's daughters. I waited to hear from God. I lay on my back, looked to the heavens, and called His name. I sat on the beach, looked in to the waters, and I called His name.

Then the Lord began to cleanse me. He got rid of the old and poured in the new. This journey is between you and God. It requires you to reach for another level. It requires you to get rid of the things that are blocking you from having a deeper relationship with God. God wants to take you to the next level.

Shortly thereafter, I began my journey of staying focused on the things of God, and being faithful to His Word. I got connected to God in a way I had never experienced before. It was then that I said to the Lord, "Lord, I want to be married, but if I'm not married, it's all right. I just want to go in my grave a Christian woman. That's all I want. If you want me to be married, you send a man. If you don't want me to be married, then I'll be comfortable with that."

Shortly after, I went to the Pancake House and there was Grainger Browning, Jr. After we got married, I struggled with the call. But, did I tell my husband that I had a call? No, because the call was between me and God.

Some things are strictly between you and God.

When I first went into ministry and even when I first came to Ebenezer, I was not embraced in ministry. Back then, women in ministry were an anomaly. I wasn't supposed to be on the pulpit. They wanted me in the third row with a hat on my head. There's nothing wrong with being a First Lady. I am a First Lady, but I'm also the co-pastor of the church. But initially, people wanted to put me in the third row, but that's not what God called me to do. It was between me and God. I struggled with that call.

When I was pregnant with our son, GT, twenty-nine years ago, the Lord brought clarity to what He wanted me to do. Shortly after I became a mother, I accepted the call. After that, almost four years later, I got pregnant again after having a miscarriage.

Seek the Lord in everything you go through in life. Ask God what you are supposed to gain out of your experiences and how you are to grow from them. There is a purpose in everything you go through.

When our daughter Candace was born, the Lord began to take me to another level in Him. When I had GT, I struggled with the call. When I miscarried, I learned to love the Lord in spite of something that was so devastating to me, and it drew me closer to Him. I needed the Lord to get me through the pain of the miscarriage. When I had my daughter, it rekindled the importance and the reality, what it means to be a woman in Christ in me.

When she was born, I was reminded of how good God was

and how far he'd brought me. This realization reinforced my faith. Everything you go through on the journey has a purpose.

I want you to hear my heart. Now it is time for you to go to the next level. The devil cannot have you.

Once you purpose in your heart that you are no longer afraid, and that you fully believe and trust God, He will give you the power to not allow your old fears to resurface in our life again. I'm not saying you'll experience fear again, but it will never stop you again because of your faithfulness and focus on God.

It's important on the journey that you're always reminded of who Jesus is, what He did for you, when He saved your soul. How it was before you were saved and what happened after you were saved. One of the things that I am gong to recommend that you do is that you remind yourself, when the enemy tries to come back again, revisit your answers to the spiritual solutions. When you get weak, when you get weary, remember that you are a faithful, focused, and fearless child of God.

SPIRITUAL SOLUTIONS

1. Stop hurting God. What is it about you, as a Christian, that grieves and hurts God that is old? You keep on doing the same thing, saying the same thing. What is it about you that you need the Lord to change?

_____

_____

_____

_____

_____

2. Get radical about your health. Exercise may not be on your change agenda, but every once in a while do something for yourself. Sisters, is there anything fitted in your closet that you used to wear, that you have to grease yourself down to slide into? Brothers, are the seams, buttons, and zippers of your favorite old suit about to pop open? Either get a size bigger or write a plan to lose some weight and exercise.

_____

_____

_____

_____

_____

3. Get inspired. Aren't you tired of repeating the same behavior? Is this the *two-thousandth time* you have apologized for the same offense? Are you ready for change? Don't you think if God can allow an African-American man to win the presidency, he'll work a miracle in your life as well? Take a cue from President Obama and write your campaign plans to effect change in your life and the lives of those around you.

_____

_____

FAITHFUL, FOCUSED & FEARLESS

_____

_____

_____

4. Separate light from darkness. Once you've committed to change your life and live righteously, you will have to make a conscious decision to change a lot of things. You'll need to be committed to changing everything in your life that you know hurts God. You'll need to change where you go, who you go with, what you do, and how you do it. What things about your life are you willing to change today?

_____

_____

_____

_____

5. Pray without ceasing. Once you decide to change your life for Christ, the enemy will attack. Be prepared. You'll need to know how and what to pray to ensure that you stay on the path to becoming a new creation in Christ. The key to your success is consistency. Write a prayer to help you keep your thoughts, words, and actions consistent with the new life you are preparing to lead.

_____

_____

_____

_____

Lesson 10

WAIT WITH AN
EXPECTANT SPIRIT

HAVE YOU BEEN waiting for God to fulfill a promise or promises that He specifically made to you at some point in your life? Do you know deep in your spirit that God has something more for you? Have you been waiting and desiring to experience a blessing from the Lord in your life?

The waiting season can be a challenge for anyone. It doesn't matter if you are a new believer, or if you've been journeying with God most of your life. To be totally honest, there are some promises that God spoke to me that I've been praying for and expecting for a long, long time. So, I understand what it feels like to wait on the Lord.

However, the waiting season gives us a unique opportunity to be honest with ourselves about the depth and strength of our faith. It's not unusual to feel uncertain and to question God while you are waiting for Him to move on your behalf. Nor is it unusual for your faith to waver while you wait. In fact, you may even find yourself wondering whether you really heard from God at all.

God wants you to confront this place of uncertainty while you're waiting for the promise, the breakthrough, or the blessing to come to be manifested in your life. He already told you that the promise was confirmed, yet your knees are buckling in the faith. You might be fulfilled in one area in your life, but there are some things in your life that are not quite going the way that you had expected.

This is a precarious place to be, this in-limbo space of unfulfilled promises and blessings, because it is fertile ground for the seed of doubt to take root in your life. This place can cause you to question the authenticity of the certainty of God. You might firmly believe that God will do just what He said He would do; but what about when the foreclosure proceedings begin, or when the divorce papers arrive, or when you lose your job? Even then, you can rest assured that whatever God promised you, no matter how long ago it was, God is going to fulfill.

We serve a God of absolute truth and certainty. We serve a God who can do anything but fail. As Christians, we must be able to wait expectantly in the posture of faith, with a certainty in our spirit during these vulnerable moments. Don't lose faith in the transitional seasons. Don't allow the waiting periods to give way to doubt.

You may very well be at your wits end. You might only be hanging on by the thinnest of threads, and you may feel yourself slipping. But you need to know that what God promised you shall come to pass. Your blessings really are on the way.

It is essential that you grasp this spiritual reality: God is majestic; He is all powerful; He is sovereign; He is the only one true living God; and, His Word is certain. Therefore, you can trust and believe that your blessings are on the way. You must be willing to hang in there just a little while longer. You must be convinced that what God promised you is near. Now is the time for you to embrace the reality of the certainty of God. In that place of doubt and questioning, right there where you've been waiting for what seems like forever, embrace the certainty of God that in due season it shall come to pass.

The Bible is full of examples of God speaking, people waiting, and the promise being fulfilled. There is always a period of time that exists between what God says and what He does. Just as our biblical ancestors remained faithful, we, too, must remain faithful, focused, and fearless during the "in between" time. We must draw closer to God and hold fast to our faith.

Instead of simply waiting passively, now is the perfect time for you to praise and worship God even more. This is your opportunity to praise Him in advance of your blessing. This is not the time for you to be irritated, annoyed, or mean-spirited. This is not the time to look like you have been sucking on lemons and drinking vinegar. This not the time for you to abandon the church, start complaining about your situation, or stop tithing. No, this is the time for you to climb up into the very face of God and get up in His space. This is the time for you to seek an intimate relationship with God. This is the time, even though you might feel like throwing in the towel and giving up, for you to seek to get to know God through Jesus Christ like you've never, ever, known Him before.

When you are in your waiting season, it's critical that you don't give in, don't get in a rut, don't get lackadaisical, and don't get doubtful. Instead, get into God's space through the Son. Now is the time for you to press all the more toward the Father through Jesus Christ, the Savior. Reclaim the intimacy with God that you once felt. Reinstate your belief in the certainty of God in your life. Reach out for God's hand, and feel His very presence. Be quiet and listen for His voice. Now is your opportunity to pursue God like you never pursued Him before. Most importantly, believe in faith as you wait on God, that His Word is certain and that what He spoke to you shall be accomplished.

You must understand that in the Word of God, a delay is not a denial. As you wait for an outpouring of God's spiritual and promised blessings in your life, you must not question God's power. Just rest in the fact that God is the source, and He endows you with resources. You can depend upon God. You can trust Him.

In Genesis 12:1–3, the Lord spoke to Abram: "Go from your country, your people and your father's household to the land I will show you. I will make you into a great nation, and I will bless you; I will make your name great, and you will be a blessing. I will bless those who bless you, and whoever curses you, I will curse; and all peoples on earth will be blessed through you."

In other words, God told Abram to separate himself from what was comfortable, familiar, convenient, and secure, and go to an unknown place to receive the promise. The promise came with a requirement. God may be requiring you to separate yourself from anyone and anything that you depend on more than you depend on God. God required Abram to separate himself from the things that were hindering his relationship with God. Abram, in his obedience to the Lord, activated his faith in God, reignited his certainty in God, and he did what was required of him. Sometimes on the faith journey, God requires you to "bust a move," and leave behind the things you rely on and do something radical for Lord. You may still be relying on mommy and daddy to meet your needs even though you're forty-five years old—bust a move. You may be relying on your significant other to make you feel whole—bust a move. You may be relying on your job to make you feel fulfilled—bust a move.

God is waiting for you to take a faith step outside of your comfort zone. I'm sure Abram may have been nervous; he was probably momentarily hesitant to leave behind all he had ever known, and he was an old man when the promise was spoken unto him. But his faith overcame his fear. God promised Abram, that if he would do what was required of him, he and all of his generations would be blessed. It was as simple and as profound as that. In other words, Abram's obedience, his faith step, not only resulted in a personal blessing, but his obedience to God resulted in a generational blessing. When God spoke, Abram went. What are you waiting for?

You can learn two important lessons from Abram:

> 1. You've got to be willing to be obedient when God speaks. When the LORD says to "bust a move," you've got to be willing to do what God says to do, even if it's uncomfortable, inconvenient, or inconceivable to others.

2. You've got to realize that your promise is bigger
than you. God spoke to Abram what He would do
not only for him, but for everyone. All the families
of the earth would be blessed by Abram's obedience.

It's time for you develop an Abram-esque attitude. Do you
believe what God has said to you? Do you trust the hand of God
on your life? Are you willing to depart, in faith, from your comfort zone? Are you willing to take a faith step?

Faith steps require hope. You're going to be uncertain, and
that's natural. Change can be scary. But, you can edify your faith
and defeat your fear with hope. Everything really is going to be
alright, because as you know, faith is the substance of things
hoped for and the evidence of things not seen. Take your faith
steps with a sense of certainty that God will make a way.

As you wait for God to fulfill the promise and blessings in
your life, you can rest in the certainty of God. Don't allow yourself to be swayed by what the situation looks like in the natural
realm. Instead, be assured that God has already worked it out in
the supernatural realm. Don't allow yourself to become confused
and confounded simply because you are at a crossroads. Hold on
to the promise. You might think time is running out, but don't
you realize that God holds time in the palm of His hand? He is
always on time.

The same God who made a promise to Abram has made a
promise to you. If you are willing to be as obedient and faithful
as Abram was, you can expect God to fulfill the promise. Abram
believed God and so should you. Your promises and blessings are
guaranteed because of the certainty of God.

The really phenomenal thing about God's promise to Abram
is because you are the seed of Abraham, you are an automatic heir
to the promise! In Galatians 3:14–16, it is written: "He redeemed
us in order that the blessing given to Abraham might come to
the Gentiles through Christ Jesus, so that by faith we might receive the promise of the Spirit. Brothers and sisters, let me take

an example from everyday life. Just as no one can set aside or add to a human covenant that has been duly established, so it is in this case. The promises were spoken to Abraham and to his seed. Scripture does not say 'and to seeds,' meaning many people, but 'and to your seed,' meaning one person, who is Christ."

Therefore, because of the covenant between God and Abraham and because of what Jesus Christ did to ensure your salvation as a believer, you are privy to the promise. Abraham has only one true seed in which the fulfillment of the promise took place, and that seed came through forty-two generations. It was Jesus Christ who was the fulfillment of the promise to Abraham's seed and who automatically made you a part of the promise.

So whatever it is that God has spoken to you, you can take it to the bank. You can be certain in faith that God will keep His promise to you. He is the same God yesterday, today, and forevermore. Hebrews 6:18 declares: "God did this so that, by two unchangeable things in which it is impossible for God to lie, we who have fled to take hold of the hope set before us may be greatly encouraged."

So if you are in Christ, when God raised His hand and made a promise to Abraham, he was making you a promise also. He promised that you would:

- be blessed
- be married
- have a new home
- receive financial blessings
- enjoy gainful employment
- receive that promotion
- carry a baby in your womb
- receive healing in your body
- see your children saved
- see your marriage restored
- see your spouse be born again

When God spoke to Abraham, He was also speaking to you, and when He raised His hand toward Abraham, He was raising

His hand toward you also. Therefore, it is done; the promise God made to you is certain. It's an established fact, and you can be sure it will be manifested in your life. When God told you He would open up the windows of heaven and pour you out blessings and give you the desires of your heart, He meant it. To doubt the promise now would be akin to telling God you simply don't believe His word. Don't allow the enemy to trick you into questioning your faith or questioning God.

So go on what you know about God. Revisit your past experiences with Him. Remember how uncompromising and unfailing He has shown Himself to be in your life thus far. When God makes a vow, unlike man, He keeps it. He carries out His word.

Be encouraged. Refuse to give up. Decide to walk by faith and not by sight. Be confident in who you are and whose you are. Know that through Jesus Christ, you are the heir to an absolute truth: What God has for you, is for you. Nothing can stop the move of God in your life.

I pray that you will use this transitional season to make your life a living testimony. Do not wait passively. Wait with an attitude of gratitude. Shake off your false sense of entitlement. Speak those things that you are waiting for as though they have already come to pass. Speak life into dead situations. Encourage others by your walk, so that they too will want to embrace the sovereignty of God. Stand boldly in faith knowing without a doubt at the end that God will do just what He said.

Know that if you don't slip and you refuse to waver, your overflow blessings will overcome you. Your breakthrough blessing will blow your mind. Your promise will come to fruition when you least expect it. All you have to do is trust and believe and hold on to the certainty of God during this waiting period. Know that while you are waiting God is perfecting you, pruning you, and maturing you so that you will be ready to receive your blessing. Don't hate the wait!

Hold on to Jesus, your big brother, the seed of Abraham, the Son of God, and the Son of Man, who took on the sins of the whole wide world. He suffered, bled, died, and overcame death so that you could receive the promise of salvation. He is the only one who got up on the third day with all power. Jesus, our eldest brother, guarantees through what He did the certainty of God.

These are the immutable facts: God will take care of you; God will provide for you; God will bless you; God will do just what He said; God will be in the midst of your struggles. You can stand on the Word of God and believe the certainty of God. Wait on the Lord and be of good courage. Wait on the Lord and renew your strength.

Throughout the Word of God, you can see that whenever God made a promise, there was also a waiting season. But He has spoken, and you definitely heard Him. So just hold on, your blessing shall come to pass.

SPIRITUAL SOLUTIONS

1. Find biblical examples of how to wait. Abraham provides a great example of how to wait in faith. Make a list of your other biblical ancestors who had to wait for the promise. Remember them as you wait on the Lord.

_____

_____

_____

_____

_____

2. Recall promises that God has already fulfilled for you. Surely this is not the first promise God has made to you. What were some of the others? How did you handle the waiting period then? What can you apply to this waiting season?

_____

_____

_____

_____

_____

3. Develop a survival plan. What will you do to keep yourself from getting discouraged during this transitional season? What activities bring you joy and elevate your attitude? How often can you do these things while you are waiting?

_____

_____

_____

_____

_____

4. Bust a move. You know God told you to leave that person, place, or thing that you rely on more than Him. Have you been obedient in "busting a move?" Why or why not?

_____

_____

_____

_____

_____

5. Honor the requirement. What has God required you to do in order for the promise to be fulfilled? Have you honored the requirement and made the necessary changes? Why or why not?

_____

_____

_____

_____

_____

Lesson 11

RECLAIM YOUR JOY

WHAT HAS STOLEN your joy? Are there any unresolved issues in your life that bring tears to your eyes when you think about it? Are there situations in your life that are weighing you down and wearing you out?

If you truly want to reclaim your joy, and you truly believe you can, then it is time for you to stand steadfast and unmovable and confront that thing which has stolen your joy. It might be a situation at your job, or a troubled relationship, or a failing marriage, or an unresolved issue with a family member. With God, you can overcome whatever has you bound or has stolen your joy—it's time to reclaim your joy.

To reclaim your joy, you've got to be willing to recognize that thing that has stolen it in the first place. You know what it is, because whenever it even crosses your mind, it brings you down, it brings tears to your eyes, and it decreases your faith reserve. It blocks you from getting closer to God. It did not happen overnight. The enemy has been stealing your joy piece by piece for years. Satan has taken something special from you and its absence saddens you and shakes your faith foundation. However, by confronting your situation, you are actively taking your circumstances before God. Give your situation to the Lord and trust and believe that He will do what He said.

You have prayed about it and you've cried about it. But God says, "Enough is enough!" It's time to reclaim your joy. God can restore your joy right now as you read, reflect, and meditate.

God wants you to understand that you must decide that you

want the spirit of joy to be restored. The joy of the Lord is your strength. Therefore, you must truly believe that weeping may endure for a night, but joy really does come in the morning. In other words, this thing that has stolen your joy has got to pass. I, too, have had to go through some things in my life that threatened to wipe me out and steal my joy.

When I was born, I weighed a little more than two pounds. The doctors declared that I would not live. But God spared my life. The enemy should've taken me out then, when I was in that incubator. I told the enemy recently and I'm telling him right now: "You will not steal my joy." Likewise, the time will come on this journey of faith when you will have to boldly proclaim: "You will not wipe me out. You cannot have my joy."

Mary, the mother of Jesus, has given us the supreme example of how to fight for our joy. Mary was a poor peasant girl who was engaged to Joseph. She was a young woman living her life in Nazareth, when Gabriel visited her. The angel Gabriel greets Mary and informs her that she is highly favored. Then Gabriel tells Mary that the Lord is with her, and she is blessed among women. Mary was troubled by this and she wondered how what Gabriel said could be true. Mary initially did not understand what Gabriel was saying to her. Her circumstances and her surroundings would not allow her to embrace what she was being told in the Lord: first, that she was highly favored; second, that the Lord was with her; and third, that she was blessed among women.

Mary had been looked upon and treated like property, and yet God identified her and spoke His blessings upon her life. Mary, like many of us, didn't see herself the way God saw her. When you don't embrace your self-worth, you can get blinded by your struggles, and miss the fact that you are favored by God.

Some people think that they are the only ones who are favored because they've attained certain positions in life. When they enter a room, they walk in and look around to see if everybody is looking at them. "Don't you see me? I am highly favored. I am the anointed one." No matter where you come from, be it the ghetto or the pinnacle of high society, we were all created in God's image. So, embrace the fact that God's favor is upon you, though not in a manner that puts others down, but in a manner that exalts the presence of God within you.

In Luke 1:30, Gabriel says, "Fear not, Mary: for thou hast found favour with God" (KJV). Maybe you need to get delivered from fear to get your joy back. Fear can bind you. Fear can lock up your emotions. Fear can hold you hostage and stop you from moving forward and prevent you from stepping into your purpose. When you are living in your purpose, you'll have unspeakable joy. When you're living outside of your purpose, you may find that you experience unhappiness, depression, and unrest.

Gabriel, in Luke 1:31, reiterates to Mary that she has found favor with God. I want to suggest that Mary's favor was connected with how she lived her life. God was pleased with her. I'm sure you've heard that favor is not fair, and I believe it to be true. I believe there is a spiritual connection between how you live your life in the sight of God and how you experience God's favor.

There are levels of favor. Mary wasn't just favored, she was "highly favored." When you are living in God's favor, God must be glorified. The favor is not upon you for you to be exalted. The favor is upon you so that God will get the glory. When God is not being glorified in the life of the one who is favored, usually the favor starts to fade. The anointing may or may not stay, the gifts may or may not operate, and the favor fades bit by bit when God is not being glorified in your life.

In Luke 1:31–33, Gabriel continues to describe to Mary what God is going to do in her life:

- She will conceive and bring forth a son
- She shall call His name Jesus.
- He shall be great.
- He shall be called the Son of the Highest.
- He shall be given the throne of His father, David.
- He shall reign over the house of Jacob forever.
- There shall be no end to His kingdom.

In considering all that Gabriel has told her, Mary questioned how this should come to pass because she was a virgin. Mary's purity of body and soul sets her up to receive God's favor. Gabriel answers her question and says:

> The Holy Spirit shall come upon thee, and the power of the Highest shall overshadow thee...the holy thing...shall be called the Son of God.
>
> —Luke 1:35, kjv

Mary found favor in God's sight because she had been purified and refined from all corruption by the overshadowing of the Holy Spirit. Gabriel confirms this supernatural event by informing Mary that her cousin, Elisabeth, who was barren and well beyond childbearing years, was six months pregnant. At this news, Mary's fear instantly turns into faith. Her doubts and her concerns turn into confidence. And Mary, this poor peasant girl, this young virgin who had been viewed as property, this young unwed mother who was engaged to Joseph, now speaks with clarity, with confidence, and with boldness: "Behold the handmaid of the Lord; be it unto me according to thy word" (Luke 1:38). And with those words, Mary surrenders totally to the will of God. You also must embrace what the Lord has spoken to you, and you must totally surrender to the will of God, so that you can reclaim your joy.

When you are waiting for God to restore your joy, it is imperative that you wait with the right spirit. Don't profess to be saved, sanctified, and filled with the Holy Spirit, and walk around with a depressed spirit. Rise above your circumstance and continue to let the joy of Jesus shine in your life. You may not feel it right away, but if you are strong enough to focus on Jesus, and not your problem, you will see your own joy restored in due season.

If God has spoken a word to you, then it is time that you proclaim it, repeat it, and rest in it. God is calling us to a place of surrender. Don't allow anything to steal your joy while you're going through and waiting on God.

The Bible records in Luke 1:39–41, that Mary went to

Elisabeth's house. When Elisabeth heard Mary's voice, her baby leapt for joy in the womb, and Elisabeth was filled with the Holy Spirit. In Luke 1:42–44, Elisabeth confirms what God has spoken when she tells her cousin Mary that she is blessed among women and blessed is the fruit of her womb. In speaking those words, Elisabeth encourages and reaffirms Mary.

Like Elisabeth, believers must encourage, confirm, and affirm each other. You know what it's like to wait on the Lord. Yet, when another believer shares his or her struggle with you, rather than give your testimony, you act like you can't relate. Instead, I encourage you to share how God brought you through your last struggle.

Luke 1:45 reads, "And blessed is she that believed: for there shall be a performance of those things which were told her from the Lord." God wants you to know that the promise He made to you shall come to pass. The thing that you've been waiting for shall be. That thing that brought sadness to your heart shall be no more. You will not shed any more tears about it, and you shall no longer suffer depression as a result of it. Your joy is about to be restored.

The same supernatural power that overshadowed Mary is the same power that shall overshadow you. The Bible declares in Luke 1:46–47, that Mary said, "My soul doth magnify the Lord, and my spirit hath rejoiced in God my Saviour." Mary recognized the reality of God's might and His mercy. He was about to turn the existing order upside down through the child in her womb. Mary's joy overcame her because the promise that God made at the beginning of time was going to be fulfilled through her womb. A peasant girl in the city of Nazareth was about to become the mother of the Savior of the world.

Just like Mary, you need to know that God will come through for you. You need to know, like Mary knew, that what God has promised, He will bring to pass. He can and He will work miracles on your behalf, if you don't get weighed down or get heavy in your soul. Remember the joy you used to have? It can be yours again. The world didn't give it to you, and the world can't take it away.

The power to reclaim your joy resides in your praise. You must continuously magnify the Lord with and rejoice in God your Savior. You shall be full of joy again. When depression tries to rear up in your heart, make a joyful noise unto the Lord. When you feel like crying, just count it all joy. God wants you to know that what you have sowed in tears, you shall reap in joy. Weeping, crying, and the gnashing of teeth may endure for a night, but joy shall come in the morning.

You must refuse to spend another day with your head hanging down with the weight of the world on your shoulders. Resist the urge to walk around looking pitiful and sad. This is not the time to give in to fatigue and defeat. No matter you are facing, just know that when the praises go up, the joy will come down. The joy of the Lord is your strength. Your joy is wrapped up in your praise. You can't praise God and be sad at the same time. You can't praise God and be depressed at the same time. If you're depressed and you start praising, you will get happy. There is a direct connection between your praise and your joy.

It's time to get your life and your thoughts together. Now is the time to discontinue your bad behavior: stay away from that other person's spouse; stop gossiping at work. If you truly want to reclaim your joy, you must move into a new place in the Lord. If you want God to fulfill His promises to you, then you must get yourself lined up with God's will. Stop doing those things that are displeasing in His sight. Get yourself together and reclaim your joy!

You cannot glorify God if you are walking around looking like you're sucking on lemons or drinking vinegar. Don't you get it? God has the power to do exceedingly abundantly above all you could ever think or imagine. (See Ephesians 3:20.) So what if your spouse left you? God has a better person for you. So what if you're still single or divorced? If God said He will give you the desires of your heart, He will. So live your life accordingly. God can give you the thing you desire the most when you least expect it. If it is ordained for you, it's for you. No demon in hell can stop what God has ordained for you. Think "reciprocity." Your joy is directly associated with how you live your life. There's a connection.

SPIRITUAL SOLUTIONS

1. Bless, encourage, and affirm others. Sharing you testimony allows you to simultaneously encourage someone else and yourself. Who needs to hear how God came through for you? Write the names of at least five people who you can encourage and the words of power that you can share with them.

_____

_____

_____

_____

_____

2. Get lyrical. Be like David and write your own praise song or poem. Write it carefully and lovingly. Don't worry about how good it is. Your goal is not to win a Grammy. Sing your praise song or read your praise poem whenever you feel your resolve growing weak.

_____

_____

_____

_____

_____

3. See yourself as God sees you. Don't get tricked into believing that you are not worthy to have your joy restored. How do you see yourself? Honestly write a description of yourself. Then re-write the description of yourself through God's eyes. Do you see the difference?

_____

_____

_____

_____

_____

4. Recall your joy. When was the last time you felt truly joyful? What was going on in your life? Write your recollection and refer to it often. Know that the joy and happiness you experienced then can be experienced again.

_____

_____

_____

_____

_____

5. Establish a plan of action. What things are you doing right now that you know are displeasing to God? Write the concrete steps you will take to change your ways and live your life in a manner that glorifies God.

_____

_____

_____

_____

_____

Scriptures to Fortify
Your Faith and
Restore Your Focus

THE WORD OF God has always been my anchor. Whenever I needed encouragement, strength, or comfort, I've always been able to turn to the scriptures to soothe my soul. Below are a few scriptures to help you along this journey of faith. I encourage you to get to know the Word. Read the Word. Meditate on it, and apply it to your life. Use the space provided to write your own scriptural references.

Genesis 1:27–28 _____

Genesis 22:14 _____

1 Kings 18 _____

Job 42:12–17 _____

The Book of Psalms _____

Proverbs 31:10–31 _____

Ecclesiastes 3:1–15 _____

Ecclesiastes 4:9–12 _____

Isaiah 40:28–31 _____

Joel 2:28–29 _____

Malachi 3:8–10 _____

Luke 1:37 _____

Luke 24 _____

John 3:16 _____

Acts 1:13–14 _____

Acts 2:1–13 _____

Romans 8 _____

Romans 12 _____

1 Corinthians 12, 13 _____

2 Corinthians 4:8–9 _____

Ephesians 1:13 _____

Philippians 4 _____

Hebrews 11 _____

Revelation 7:9–17 _____

EPILOGUE

THROUGHOUT MY JOURNEY of faith, I have experienced the dichotomy of life. People may think that because I am a co-pastor, somehow I am exempt from life's struggles. However, just like you, I have enjoyed victorious, glorious moments in my life; and I've also experienced difficulties and trials. I did not become a faithful, focused, and fearless woman of God overnight. My strength is a direct result of a culmination of all my life experiences. My strength comes from the Lord.

Through it all, I really learned that God is an authentic, miracle-working God. I learned that His love for me is beyond human comprehension. I learned the importance of dialoguing with God. It is through constant, consistent communication with Him that I am able to live faithful, focused, and fearless. There are few things that are certain in this life:

- Faith and faithfulness are a must.
- Focusing on the things of God is essential.
- Fearlessness of anything that is evil and contrary to the things of God is mandatory.

If nothing else, I pray that these lessons have inspired you to seek God diligently. I pray that you thirst for Him. I pray that you honor Him by the way you live your life. I pray that you revere His awesome majesty. I pray that you never, ever back up from pursuing the promises He has spoken to you.

I pray you live a life, through the power of our Lord Jesus Christ, that is faithful, that is focused, and that is fearless.

God bless you.

Notes

Lesson 3
1. Karl Barth, *Church Dogmatics* (Peabody, MA: Hendrickson Publishers, 2010).

ABOUT THE AUTHOR

R EVEREND DR. Jo Ann Browning is co-pastor of Ebenezer African Methodist Episcopal Church in Fort Washington, Maryland. She is married to the Reverend Dr. Grainger Browning, Jr., who is the senior pastor. She is the very proud mother of two young adults, Grainger III (married to Courtney Riley Browning) and Candace. She is the proud grandmother of Kaylah Jo Ann Browning and Grainger Browning IV.

Rev. Dr. Browning graduated from Boston University in 1976 with a Bachelor of Science Degree in Communications. She received a Master of Divinity Degree in 1986 and a Doctorate of Ministry from Howard University School of Divinity in 1991. She was a recipient of the Benjamin E. Mays Fellowship and the Pew Fellowship. She also holds an honorary Doctorate of Divinity from African Methodist Episcopal University in Monrovia, Liberia, West Africa.

Rev. Browning accepted the call to preach in 1982 at Hemmingway Memorial A.M.E. Church, Chapel Oaks, Maryland, and for nine months in 1983, she served on the ministerial staff at St. Paul A.M.E. Church in Cambridge, Massachusetts. When her husband was appointed to pastor Ebenezer A.M.E. Church in 1983, she served with him in ministry and the church had seventeen members and a $12,000 budget. In 1998, after serving for fifteen years as a full-time assistant minister, assistant pastor and co-pastor with her husband who is the senior pastor, Bishop Vinton R. Anderson, presiding prelate of the Second Episcopal District, gave her an appointment as co-pastor of the Ebenezer A.M.E. Church. This unprecedented appointment officially recognized the Brownings as a pastoral team. Subsequently, their present Bishop, Presiding Prelate of the Second Episcopal District, Bishop Adam Jefferson Richardson, has continued to give her the appointment as co-pastor of Ebenezer A.M.E. Church for eleven years. Ebenezer's membership is ten thousand with one hundred ministries and a budget of $10 million.

In addition to her responsibilities at Ebenezer, Pastor Jo Ann Browning has had the opportunity to preach, teach, and facilitate workshops throughout the United States, Haiti, Bermuda, Barbados, Germany, Israel, Liberia, and South Africa. In July 2002, Rev. Dr. Jo Ann Browning was inducted into Delta Sigma Theta Sorority, Incorporated as an honorary member.

In 2006, she founded Journey of Faith, LLC, a company dedicated to empowering women. Her first book, *Our Savior, Our Sisters, Ourselves: Biblical Teachings & Reflections on Women's Relationships*, published in 2006, became an *Essence Magazine* bestseller. The book provides teachings that explore the realities of being a black woman, wife, mother, and minister. It is designed to empower and bless women as they continue on their journeys of faith.

Rev. Dr. Jo Ann Browning is grateful for the opportunity to share these lessons that she received from the Lord with all women of God, regardless of race. In all that has been said and done, she continuously gives God all the praise, honor, and glory for the opportunity to be a humble servant of her Lord and Savior Jesus Christ!

Contact the Author

Websites
www.ebenezerame.org and www.drjabrowning.com

Email
jb@ebenezerame.org

Telephone
301–265–8210

Mail
Journey of Faith LLC
938 E. Swan Creek Rd., #264
Fort Washington, MD 20744

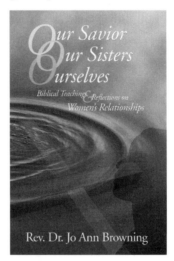